The Self-Sufficiency Garden

The Self-Sufficiency Garden

Feed your family and save money

HUW RICHARDS
SAM COOPER

Contents

Foreword

Don't you need a lot of growing space to be self-sufficient? Won't it take up too much time? Surely you'll need to buy in lots of compost, which kind of defeats the point, and doesn't the hungry gap make it impossible anyway? Less than two years ago I would have answered "yes" to all those questions.

But that negative attitude really bothered me. I wanted so badly to prove that aiming for self-sufficiency was possible that I just had to find out for myself. The fact that I am writing this book is a bit of a giveaway, but I can happily say that the answer to those same questions is now a definite "no".

The Self-Sufficiency Garden is a book that captures the journey I went on. I've turned my own experience into a detailed plan for growing food year-round that is both practical and achievable. It is crammed with useful tips as well as lessons I learned along the way, and I hope it will help you take a significant step closer to your goal of self-sufficiency.
Huw

So you want to grow an abundance of fresh food? But then what? If you are aiming for self-sufficiency, it's vital to make the most of your harvests and ensure you have enough to see you through the leaner months.

Therefore, unlike cookery books, this one places the kitchen purely in service to the garden. It will help you unlock and capture all the flavours of your fresh, homegrown produce, give you ideas for cooking and preserving your harvests, and, most importantly, do it as efficiently as possible so there's plenty of time to enjoy your garden.

The Self-Sufficiency Garden combines Huw's growing skills with my own experience in the kitchen as a trained chef. It is my hope that it will give you the confidence to aim for year-round self-sufficiency, and in a way that fits in with your busy day-to-day lives.
Sam

Principles of a Self-Sufficiency Garden

A space that will provide you with sustainably grown, affordable produce every day of the year is based on three fundamental considerations: nutrition, time, and cost. Once you've understood their importance, the journey towards self-sufficiency can begin.

We've designed the garden to produce a significant amount of nourishing food from a space measuring just 10 x 12.5m (33 x 43ft). The approach is practical and efficient because we incorporate time- and cost-saving measures at every stage of the process, from choosing the best crop varieties to efficient growing and food prep. Follow our methods and you'll save time and money in the garden, as well as in the kitchen. The simple diagram (right) shows our priorities.

A simple pyramid illustrates the three key principles of self-sufficiency gardening – nutrition, cost, and time – with nutrition at the top.

PRINCIPLE PYRAMID

Nutrition is at the top of the pyramid because our key aim is to produce nutrient-rich, homegrown food from healthy soil in the space available. At the base, forming the foundation, are time and cost – principles and priorities and must also be taken into consideration. Guided by these three principles, we'll show you how to organize your time more efficiently to achieve optimum homegrown nutritious crops for the lowest cost. Now let's look at each of the principles in more detail.

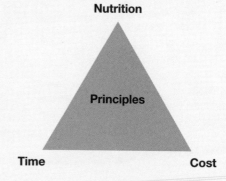

Nutrition

Principles

Time   Cost

Time

Considering time as a resource that we can only spend once helps us to prioritize. It encourages us to get as much achieved as possible, which brings satisfaction. Understanding the importance of time-management and prioritization also helps us to avoid bottlenecks and celebrate each step of the journey. Embrace seasonality and the changes that come with it, and always view gardening tasks through the lens of opportunity.

PUTTING PRINCIPLES INTO PRACTICE

Together, the three key principles constitute our guiding ethos as we work towards becoming self-sufficient. Whenever there is a decision to be made, bear them in mind and ask yourself how your decision might align with one or more of these principles, and how you could maximize its benefits. Once you have embraced the principles, you can make use of the two approaches we explain in detail on the next page. These will help keep you on track so you can enjoy success with your growing as soon as possible.

Nutrition

Prioritizing soil health is key to creating a productive and resilient garden. Living soil that is rich in beneficial microbial life enables plants to access vital nutrients and flourish. We then absorb those nutrients when we take our fresh garden produce into the kitchen to prepare and cook it. We interact with them via our tastebuds and sense of smell. And the more nutritious the food is, the better it's going to taste. Good nutrition is essential for our own health and wellbeing, as well as that of the plants in our gardens.

Cost

Making the most of free and low-cost resources from your local area is the best way to reduce your dependency on material sourced from further afield. The same applies to material sourced on a regular basis. You can, for example, create raised beds from salvaged material such as pallets, establish a composting scheme in your community, and trade (barter) your skills or your equipment with other people. Growing food in this way means you are sure to spend less, which will save you money at the local shop or supermarket.

> **I believe that any time you eat something you have grown yourself, it's a valid reason for celebration.**

SELF-SUFFICIENCY APPROACHES

The goal of self-sufficiency is one for the long term and it's vital to keep yourself motivated as you continue your journey towards it. Keeping track of progress and knowing you're heading in the right direction is key, as is celebrating all the small successes that get you closer to your goal.

Two approaches to self-sufficiency have worked well for me – incremental and crop-focused – are explained in detail below. Using the first, you break the self-sufficiency journey down into simple, achievable stages, such as your first meal with all vegetables homegrown. Then each stage takes you one step further down the road to self-sufficiency.

With the second approach, the aim is to be self-sufficient in a specific crop over one growing season. Once you've achieved this you build on your success by adding another crop.

1. Incremental self-sufficiency
Starting with an ambitious target, such as not buying vegetables and only eating homegrown and preserved produce, is only achievable if you break the process

down incrementally and build momentum over the long term. Rather like training for a marathon, you don't run all 26 miles on day one. It's easier to take it in stages, starting with half a mile, then building up to a point where you feel ready to tackle the big event.

Below are some key stages, each one will bring your goal a little closer, and each is a cause for celebration:

- ⌄ First meal including homegrown veg
- ⌄ First meal where all the veg is homegrown
- ⌄ First day where all the veg you eat is homegrown
- ⌄ First weekend where all the veg you eat is homegrown
- ⌄ First week where all the veg you eat is homegrown
- ⌄ First fortnight...
- ⌄ First month...
- ⌄ First season...
- ⌄ First year!

Setbacks are a fact of life so if you encounter problems or you need a break, don't be tempted to push on to the next stage. It's better to

stick with what you have achieved, such as eating homegrown veg one day a week, until you feel comfortable moving on.

2. Crop-focused self-sufficiency
Unlike the incremental approach, your target here is self-sufficiency in a single crop, for example salad or garlic, over one season. Deciding to eat only homegrown salad over summer or grow enough garlic to last you all winter does involve a specific timeframe. However, focusing on just one crop is certainly easier than thinking about everything that's growing in your whole garden. As time progresses and productivity increases, you'll be confident enough to add more ambitious targets for each new growing season, such as eating homegrown potatoes all year round.

TIP
Among the best crops to start with for a quick win are perennial and annual herbs, such as rosemary and parsley. They don't need much space, grow very easily, preserve well, and a little goes a long way!

Creating the Garden

Garden Overview

Now you're familiar with the principles of modern-day self-sufficiency, the next step is to create the space that makes it all possible. Then once your garden is set up, it's time to start sowing ready for a highly productive and enjoyable growing year.

SIZE AND YIELD

When developing the self-sufficiency garden, we set ourselves the goal of producing 365kg (805lb) of food over one year. This works out at 1kg per day between two adults or three portions each of your recommended five a day.

It took just 5 months from the first sowings in early March to harvest 200kg (440lb) or 2,500 portions of fresh food. It was all grown in a garden measuring approximately 10m x 12.5m, which is exactly the same size as half an allotment plot. With a total growing area of just 75sq m (excluding paths), we aimed for a yield of around 5kg (11lb) of produce for every square metre. Within 200 days from the first sowings, we hit the 365kg goal – five months ahead of target! Now we're sharing exactly the same formula we used to achieve these incredible yields.

Adapting for your garden

Your plot will probably be laid out very differently from the self-sufficiency garden, which was designed and purpose-built to fit the allocated space. But you can still include many of the key growing spaces by slotting them in around what is already there. If you are new to gardening, take it slowly and introduce just two or three spaces during the first growing season to build confidence.

When creating a garden from scratch, I would urge you to prioritize under cover growing by establishing a hot bed or hoop beds. This will extend your growing season and give you a wider choice of crops. Secondly, build two or three raised beds for growing staples such as potatoes and onions. Thirdly, set up at least one compost bin so you can start improving your soil's fertility.

In this chapter, I'll show you how to create each of the garden's growing spaces.

Raised Beds

Raised beds are the "bones" of the self-sufficiency garden. By dividing up the outside planting area into smaller sections, rather than growing in one large block, managing the space becomes much easier. For valuable under cover growing space, we've modified some of the beds into hoop beds by adding a hooped frame and top cover.

SIZE AND ASPECT

With raised beds (pictured opposite), there is always a balance to strike in terms of size. Ideally, your bed should be as big as possible, but without being awkward to access. Too long, and you'll be tempted to jump over rather than walk round it; too wide and you'll have to step into the bed to reach the middle. Over the years, I've found the ideal size to be no longer than 3m (10ft), and no wider than 1.2 m (4ft). Beds in the polytunnel, however, can be wider. The under cover growing space is so valuable that I'm more than happy to reach over the beds a little further when planting and harvesting. One long side should face south (see p26 for more on aspect).

SIDES

Sturdy materials, such as wood or blocks for the sides, give each bed a clearly defined boundary. These offer seating and the option to attach trellis. A bed with sides also allows for a greater growing depth, especially if your ground lacks topsoil. Solid sides, too, will stop weeds encroaching from paths. However, a simple heaped bed without a frame is the most affordable option, and it's a good choice as long as there is at least 20cm (8in) of topsoil below the surface.

FILLING YOUR BED

Add enough topsoil to come two-thirds of the way up the bed, then fill the top third

KEYHOLE RAISED BED

Perfect for increasing the growing area in corners or against boundaries, these beds have a central access path. See the salad bed on the plan on page 43.

with compost. If this is in short supply, you can get away with just a 5cm (2in) layer of compost, forked in with the top layer of topsoil. Alternatively, fill beds over time by treating them a bit like a shallow compost bin. Add material you'd usually put in the compost bin, including leaves, grass clippings, used coffee grounds, plus shredded cardboard, then finish with a layer of compost over the top as a growing medium. Over time the material will break down and provide nutrients for future planting.

Tip

Hügelkultur *(mound culture) is a system that relies on different layers of organic material breaking down over time. It's an effective and low-cost option for filling deep raised beds.*

PATHS

These should be wide enough to allow for crouching down between beds to carry out routine tasks, or to push a wheelbarrow along. In the self-sufficiency garden, I've opted to mostly use buckets instead of a wheelbarrow and chosen a minimum path width of 40cm (16in). The main access route (from the gate to the polytunnel), however, is at least 60cm (2ft) wide. If these dimensions aren't suitable for your plot, work out the most appropriate path width by using two planks of wood and a tape measure.

My go-to material for paths is woodchip. It not only looks smart and offers good grip but is also light to move around and allows water to drain. The woodchip also feeds the beneficial microbial life in the soil.

HOOP BEDS

Hoop beds are essentially raised beds with a "hoop house", a mini-polytunnel, on top. They are filled in the same way. Providing fantastic under cover growing space outside, these beds are designed to produce early harvests as well as late-season crops. I'm sharing how to make a 3m (10ft) x 1.2m (4ft) hoop house, which works in my space but you can adjust the width to suit. I used standard lengths of timber and plastic sheeting to make the hoop house then attached it to the raised bed frame with hinges along one side so it could be opened (see below) for easy access.

Kit list

3 x 3m lengths of 2 x 3 timber

2 x 3m lengths of 25mm x 50mm roofing batten

2 x 1.2m lengths of 2 x 3 timber

2 x 60cm lengths of 2 x 3 timber

8 x 3m lengths of 22mm-thick alkathene pipe

3 stainless steel door hinges

5m x 2m UV plastic sheeting

80mm stainless steel screws

40mm stainless steel screws

2.4m total length of thin wood strips (any lengths)

Nails (longer than the wood strips)

Tools

Hammer

Wood saw

Tape measure

Pencil

Drill

25mm drill bit

1. Assemble materials and tools, cutting timber to correct size if necessary.

2. Make the frame by laying the 2 x 3m timbers and the 2 x 1.2m timbers on a flat surface to form a rectangle. With the wider sides of the wood facing upwards, use 80mm screws to join the corners together securely.

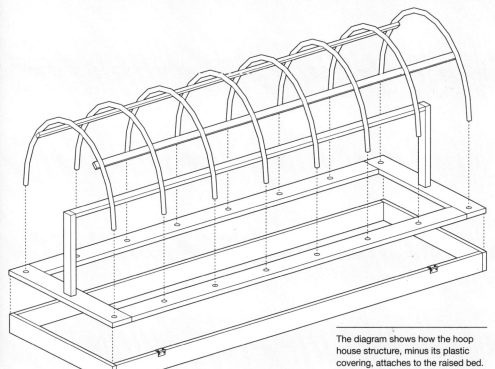

The diagram shows how the hoop house structure, minus its plastic covering, attaches to the raised bed. Hinges on one side allow it to open.

3. Stand the 2 x 60cm timbers vertically at the mid-point of each narrow end of the rectangle. With the wider side of the wood facing outwards, use 80mm screws to attach each firmly to the frame, directly on top in the centre. To complete the frame, screw the third 3m length of timber to the two uprights, and ensure it is flush with the top.

4. Use 40mm screws to fix the 2 hinges, one at 1m and the other at 2m, along the long side of the hoop house structure. Now attach the hinges to the long side of the raised bed.

5. Before fitting the lengths of pipe for the hoops, make 8 holes along each 3m side of the frame using the 25mm drill bit. Drill a hole approx 5cm from each end then space the remaining 6 holes around 42cm apart.

6. Insert the 8 x 3m lengths of pipe into the holes and bend to create hoops over the frames. Screw through the top of the frame and the pipe to hold the hoops firmly in place.

7. Now attach each 3m length of roofing batten halfway up each hooped side to strengthen the

frame. Ensure the batten is on the inside of the hoops and runs lengthwise, then attach it by screwing through the pipes.

8. To attach the plastic cover, first lay the sheet over the hoop frame, ensuring all sides are equal. Next, nail each of the thin wood strips to the plastic along both sides and around both ends so it's securely attached all the way round the base of the frame. It may be easier to work with a partner as you move around the hoop house, pulling the plastic taut as you go.

Hot Beds

"A hot bed is a warmed, protected environment, created by heat generated from decomposing organic matter, used for producing early crops".
Jack First, author of **Hot Beds**

One of the most productive, methods for growing food in a small space, a hot bed allows you to harvest veg from March and April that would usually crop in June and July. It consists of two frames: a simple outer one to hold the organic material together, and the inner growing frame that protects the seedlings and retains heat. On top of the inner frame sit two "windows" to let in light (pictured opposite). These are not fixed and can be removed. Detailed step-by-step instructions for building the inner growing frame are given on page 24. Hot beds also double up as compost bins, so at the end of the

season you will have a huge volume of material for mulching your raised beds.

Outer frame
The ideal size for the outer frame of the hot bed is 1.5 x 1.5m (5 x 5ft), and you can make it from inexpensive or free scrap wood, such as pallets, old fencing, and scaffold boards. It's a good idea to add ratchet straps or support stakes. These will prevent the outer frame from bulging outwards when it's been filled.

Inner frame
This is smaller, ideally 1.2 x 1.2m (4 x 4ft). I recommend building it from 2.5cm- (1in-) thick wood for durability. On

top are the two windows, known as lights, and you simply wedge each one open with a piece of wood to provide ventilation on warm days. The lights need to be kept securely in place during windy weather, and a simple solution is to attach a bungee cord using U nails.

Filling the bed
Traditionally, a mix of horse manure and straw was used to fill hot beds, usually in a 50:50 ratio of half brown material (straw) and half green (manure). Seaweed, grass clippings, and farmyard manure can all be substituted for horse manure, and woodchip, shredded cardboard, and

spent hay, for straw. Add them in thin alternate layers and in the half brown/half green ratio. Try to get hold of ramial woodchip (from tree branches less than 7cm/2¾ in) in diameter). It's the ideal material because it contains 75 per cent of the tree's minerals. Use it alone to generate heat: no need to add other ingredients.

As you add layers of material to the bed, walk over it. This helps to reduce air pockets and ensure the temperature of the hot bed stays relatively constant over a prolonged period. After filling the bed to the desired height (see table below), soak with a hose until water runs out from the base, add a 8–10cm (3–4in) layer of compost on top, and leave for 2–3 days for temperatures to settle. Now place the growing frame, minus the lights, on top, pushing it 3–4cm (1¼–1½in) into the compost, and fill the inside with an additional 8cm (3in) layer of compost before placing the lights on top. This will leave only a small space for growing, but smaller volumes of air will heat up more quickly. As your seedlings grow, gently lift the growing frame up bit by bit to create a little more internal space.

The depth to which the bed is filled will determine for how long it retains heat.

Depth of material	Heat generated for
80–90cm (32–36in)	3 months
60–70cm (24–28in)	2 months
35–45cm (14–18in)	1 month

I add corner posts to strengthen the outer frame (above). Once the frame is filled, the manure and straw are thoroughly soaked (left).

Follow instructions on how to construct the inner growing frame (above) and the lights (right and below) overleaf.

MAKE THE INNER GROWING FRAME

Materials

Letters correspond to lengths of wood as shown on the diagram opposite. Use wood 2.5cm (1in) thick; it will help retain heat and last longer.

G / F	115cm x 10cm
I	110cm x 10cm
H	110cm x 10cm
D	115cm x 20cm
C	115cm x 20cm
B	120cm x 20cm
A	120cm x 20cm
E	120cm x 10cm
J	Two back-end pegs 30cm 2x2
K	Two front-end pegs 20cm 2x2

For the frame

1 x plank 115 x 10cm for F+G

2 x 110 x 10cm planks for H+I

2 x planks 115 x 20cm for C+D

2 x planks 120 x 20cm for A+B

1 x plank 120 x 10cm for E

4 x pegs: 2 x 30cm (J); 2 x 20cm (K), made from 2 x 2 wood

4–5cm stainless steel screws

2 galvanized U-nails (staples)

For each light

2 x 130cm lengths of 2 x 2 wood

2 x 50cm lengths of 2 x 2 wood

1 plank 40 x 5cm

2 x thin planks 60 x 5cm

2 x thin planks 110 x 5cm

1 x sheet of 80 x 200cm polytunnel plastic

8cm stainless steel screws

5cm stainless steel screws

Tools

Bungee cord

Saw

Drill

Screwdriver

Hammer

Scissors or utility knife

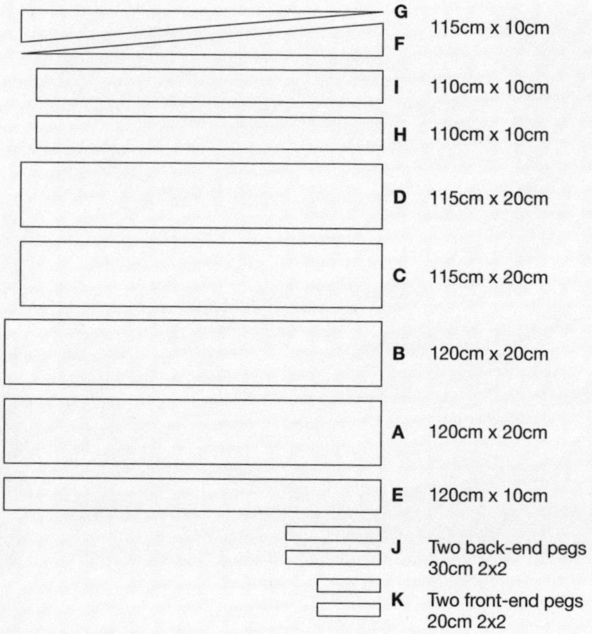

For the frame

1. Cut the plank for F and G diagonally to create 2 triangles.

2. Create the base of the growing frame by screwing the 2 x 20cm (8in) pegs to either end of plank A, and the 2 taller 30cm (12in) pegs to either end of plank B.

3. Attach each end of planks C and D to the pegs you screwed to planks A & B to make a rectangular frame.

4. Screw each end of plank E to one of the 30cm (12in) taller pegs at the back.

5. Screw the short edge of each triangular piece of wood, F and G, to the taller 30cm (12in) pegs. Measure 10cm (4in) in from the narrowest end of each and attach a screw down into the plank below to secure.

6. Screw planks H and I to the sloping sides at the same slant and with a 5cm (2in) lip above, 2.5cm (1in) in from either end.

7. Hammer in a U-nail just in from the top end at the mid-point of plank C to form an eye for the bungee cord. Hammer in another U-nail in the corresponding position on the outside of plank D.

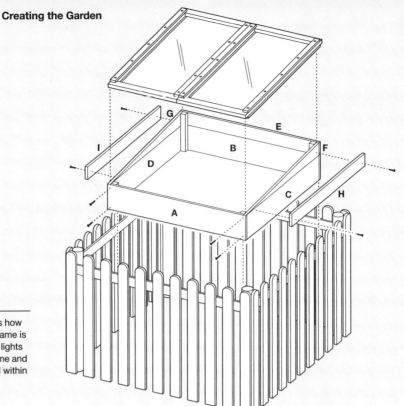

This diagram shows how the inner growing frame is assembled and the lights sit on top. Both frame and lights are contained within the outer frame.

For the light

1. Attach the 2 50cm 2 x 2 lengths to both ends of the 2 130cm 2 x 2s using the 8cm screws to make a rectangle.

2. Screw the smaller 40cm plank onto the inside of one of the 50cm 2 x 2 sections so that half of its width protrudes, using the 5cm screws. This acts as a lip to stop the light sliding down the growing frame (pictured on p23, top right).

3. With the lip on the underside, lay the polytunnel plastic on top so there is an equal overhang of plastic at each end.

4. Place the thin 60cm plank at the very top of the plastic sheet (the lip end), pull the plastic sheet around it and roll it up and around 4–5 times towards you (pictured on p23, below left). Then screw the plank flush with the outer edge of the 60cm 2 x 2, using 5cm screws at equal spacings (pictured on p23, below right).

5. Place the second thin 60cm plank at the other end of the plastic sheet, and roll it up, as before. The plastic will tighten as you move towards the 60cm 2 x 2, but give it an extra turn or two so the sheet is as taut as possible. Now screw the plank to the outer

edge of the 60cm 2 x 2 using 5cm screws at equal spacings.

6. To keep the long sides of the plastic in place, screw 2 x 110cm planks along the top of both the 130cm 2 x 2s (lip is still underneath), using 5cm screws at equal spacings. Trim off the excess plastic.

7. Repeat the process for the second light.

8. Place both lights directly on top of the inner growing frame. They should fit snugly.

Polytunnel

Offering a sheltered, undercover environment, a polytunnel is a plot's most precious growing area and significantly increases the range of crops gardeners in temperate climates can grow. I use mine through all four seasons, from starting off seedlings in spring to picking fresh salad leaves in winter, out of the cold and rain.

SIZE AND ASPECT

In the garden we have a 6 x 3m (20 x 10ft) polytunnel. This size is not only ample for growing a large volume of food, but is also in proportion to the external raised beds. The width allows for a single pathway down the middle with two 1.2m- (4ft-) wide beds either side. These raised beds are built and filled in exactly the same way as outdoor raised beds (see p16), and I would also recommend increasing the proportion of compost (and therefore of organic matter) to 50 per cent so the soil retains as much moisture as possible. During hot weather, polytunnel beds can dry out quickly if the surface is not protected by plants or mulch.

In terms of aspect, the polytunnel should match that of your raised beds and run along an east/west axis. In summary, one long side faces south, with one end facing west and the other facing east.

PURCHASE AND CONSTRUCTION

The vast majority of polytunnels are purchased in kit form and comprise a metal frame, wooden doors, and plastic sheeting to cover. There are also numerous different types of foundation to suit your ground. All good polytunnel suppliers should provide clear guidance as to which tunnel specification will be most suitable for your site, and each polytunnel will come with clear instructions on how to assemble. You will need at least one extra person to lend a hand with construction; alternatively many polytunnel companies offer assembly for an extra cost. You could also contract a local builder to carry out the assembly.

WATERING

Hand watering, using several cans or standing by a hose, takes time as well as energy. To make the job easier, I recommend installing soaker hoses in the polytunnel. This can be done either before or after the beds have been planted up, then all you need to do is turn on the tap (and then remember to turn it off!). For maximum efficiency and to reduce evaporation, bury the hose just under the surface of the beds. Watering is best done early in the morning or late in the afternoon. Two to three sessions of 35–40 minutes a week with the soaker hose should be ample for your polytunnel crops.

WINTER BENEFITS

A polytunnel won't just provide an abundance of summer favourites, such as tomatoes. With careful planning it can also be amazingly productive in winter, when you could be harvesting fresh greens and salad leaves. Check out page 109 for how you can produce abundant fresh produce during the dark months and into spring. The polytunnels' shelter and ambient temperature also helps overwinter less hardy plants.

Potting Bench and Tool Storage

The place where seeds are sown in modules and potted on, the potting bench is the hub of the garden. Making your own bench is straightforward, and by adding simple shelving beneath you can also store the most useful tools and garden accessories, from trowels and secateurs to seed trays and labels.

POTTING BENCH

I've found that a simple, inexpensive homemade trestle table makes a fantastic potting bench. Mine consists of two A-frame trestles with two planks laid over the top to create a sturdy work surface. The potting bench is also lightweight and easily moved by one person.

To cut down on spillage when sowing and potting on, I keep a large, flexible trug filled with compost on top of the bench. Alternatively, a strong cardboard box with the height of one side reduced also makes a good temporary potting tray. Simply replace the box after three to four weeks.

Kit list

8 x 67cm lengths of 2 by 3 timber	
8 x 90cm lengths of 2 by 3 timber	
4 x metal hinges and screws	
32 x 7–10cm screws	
Planks to lay on top	

1. To make one of the four "frames", screw two of the long and short pieces of timber together as indicated (see diagram). Repeat to make four frames.

2. Screw a hinge to the top centre of one frame and join it to the second frame. When joined the two "legs" open up to create a trestle. Repeat for the third and fourth frames.

3. Place the two trestles apart then lay planks on top for the work surface.

Storing trays and pots

You can create very simple shelves under the potting bench using old scaffold boards and breeze blocks. Place a block at either end, lay a plank on top and repeat. You now have a sturdy shelving unit for all your seed trays, module trays, and pots.

Seedling area

Once you have sown seeds in module trays and pots, you will need a space where the seedlings can germinate and grow on. I recommend buying a mini-greenhouse with wire or mesh shelving, and placing it next to the potting bench. Alternatively, if space or funds are really tight, tie a wire shelf to the roof of the polytunnel and hang it above a raised bed.

TOOLS

Having a dedicated space for tools, so you don't waste time looking for them, leads to greater efficiency. I use an old shoe rack for hand tools and keep it under the potting bench. Long-handled tools can be stored upright in the space between the potting bench and the polytunnel end. I've put together a list of tools and accessories that I find essential (see right).

Key hand tools and accessories

Trowel
Hand fork
Pocket knife
Garden scissors
Secateurs
Garden twine
Labels
Pen and pencil
Notepad
Gloves
Hand hoe
Brush

Long-handled tools

Shears
Shovel
Fork
Rake
Oscillating hoe or push-pull hoe

This diagram shows the positions of the screws for each pair of legs, as well as the hinges. The three planks sit on top.

Watering Station

A simple watering station – one that is easy to use and accessible at a moment's notice – is, to my mind, a good watering station. The key element is a reliable water supply. In the self-sufficiency garden, we've opted for a straightforward set-up with plenty of storage capacity.

WATER SOURCE

Firstly, establish the source of your supply. Most households and allotments have access to mains water, but water is a finite resource so do collect rainwater at every opportunity. Divert water that runs off shed, house, greenhouse, and garage roofs into water butts. You could even set up a large tarpaulin to collect water during heavy showers.

WATER STORAGE

Stored water is one of the most important resources for the self-sufficiency garden, especially during periods of very dry weather or even hosepipe bans. Aim to have at least 500 litres (50 full 10-litre/2.2 gallon watering cans) of water in reserve for emergencies. For both convenience and cost-saving I use IBC (intermediate bulk container) tanks (pictured right) that store 1,000 litres (220 gallons). You can even stack one on top of the other to double storage capacity from the same footprint. If you don't have mains water, attach your hose to the top tank for gravity-assisted flow, and keep the bottom tank as your reserve.

Dual-purpose storage

We use the metal cage of the IBC tank as a trellis to grow climbing beans. It looks good, plants benefit from the heat retained by the water overnight, and you can add "S" hooks to hang watering equipment from.

Hose set-up

I recommend investing in a 20m (65ft) hosepipe so you can reach all parts of the garden. Attaching a wall- or fence-mounted hosepipe reel will save space and also prevent you from tripping over hosepipe all summer. One multi-spray nozzle should be sufficient, provided there is a good "soaker" setting for mature plants, as well as a "gentle" setting for just after sowing and for seedlings.

Dunk barrel

Fill your watering can by dunking it in a pre-filled barrel for couple of seconds rather than waiting for the hose. Attaching a water stopper to the inlet will also prevent overflowing when refilling. To save on cost, a heavy-duty recycled plastic waste bin with a lid is easily sourced and makes an inexpensive alternative to a barrel.

Watering cans

When you don't want to unroll the hose, 2 x 10-litre (2-gallon) watering cans allow for easy watering of a small area. These are also needed for applying liquid feeds and amendments (see pp208–211).

Planks

Keep a few 1m (3ft) planks (mine are from pallets) at the watering station to lay over rows of direct-sown seeds to retain moisture. Letting soil dry out leads to sporadic germination, so I use this "plank method" with direct-sown crops such as salads, carrots, parsnips, and swede, immediately after watering. Remove the plank once you notice the first seedlings emerge.

Boundaries and Vertical Growing

Put simply, most gardens have a rectangular-shaped boundary offering four different growing aspects: north-, south-, east- and west-facing. It's important to understand the benefits of each before deciding which crop will be most productive when grown up against which boundary, using trellis or simple structures. When choosing crops, I follow a simple planting guide, set out in the table below.

Aspect	Light and warmth	Suitable crops
South-facing	Full sun, warm	Squash, tomatoes, fruit trees, trailing berries, perennial Mediterranean herbs, beans, peas
East-facing	Morning sunlight, cooler afternoons	Soft fruit, salads, annual herbs
West-facing	Afternoon sunlight, warm evenings	Soft fruit, perennial veg, edible flowers
North-facing	Shady and cool	Leafy greens (providing sky not obscured by overhanging trees)

Aspect variations
Many boundaries aren't perfectly aligned with one of the four aspects. Where, for example, a garden has a southwest- or southeast-facing boundary, I treat them as south-facing because both will receive sun for the greater part of the day.

Rabbit-proofing boundaries
Use purpose-made wire fencing right around the perimeter, burying it 30cm (12in) below ground level to deter rabbits. Alternatively, bend the bottom 30cm (12in) of fencing outwards from the base then cover with a light layer of soil. Rabbits always burrow up

against the boundary, and using either method means they will immediately encounter a wire barrier.

TRELLIS AND SIMPLE STRUCTURES

If your garden has only wire fencing right around the boundary, you can still create a growing surface at the back of a south-facing border to retain warmth and add shelter. For a low-cost solution, invest in some sheets of garden trellis then attach them securely along the fence. The additional height will allow you to grow and train taller plants, such as blackberries or a small apple tree.

Vertical value
After under cover growing space, vertical space is incredibly valuable because it supplements your growing area. For example, you can attach deep guttering to fences at the back of borders and grow salads there, freeing up bed space for crops that need more root space. Make simple supports, such as A-frames (pictured below), wigwams, and mini-fences, to support tall-growing plants such as peas and beans. Trailing squashes, such as pumpkins, can quickly take over large areas of ground but these can also be be trained vertically and will fruit well. In the polytunnel, you can easily suspend hanging baskets from the structure to grow bush tomatoes or strawberries.

Cold frame
A cold frame is a useful additional space for starting off seeds in modules and for holding potted plants until ready for transplanting.

Homemade Compost

Turning waste material into compost produces a beautiful, rich growing resource that is essential for the crops in your garden to thrive. Making your own, and not buying it in, is one of the best things you can do to create a more resilient garden.

ANNUAL COMPOST REQUIREMENT

Excluding containers and hot beds, the self-sufficiency garden has just under 70sq m (700sq ft) of beds. On average, these need a 3cm (1¼in) layer of compost applied annually at the end of the growing season). This ensures sufficient organic matter and nutrition for the high yields expected and equates to a compost requirement of 2,100 litres (460 gallons). Most of this quantity can be fulfilled by the material in the two hot beds, once they have been emptied (pictured left). From the three compost bays I recommend, you'll have enough material

to make up the shortfall, as well as fill containers, create your own seed/potting compost blends, and even produce a small surplus to use as a bartering resource.

Compost calculations
To fill a hot bed requires 2,000 litres (44 gallons) of organic materia. Assuming it loses just over half of its mass during decomposition, you will be left with 1,000 litres (220 gallons).

To mulch (pictured above) 1sq m (1sq ft) of growing space with a 3cm- (1¼-in) deep layer of compost requires 30 litres (6½ gallons) of compost.

Bin size
A compost bin should be at least 1 cubic metre (3 cubic feet) to allow heat to build up and then be retained in the core for efficient decomposition. It will produce enough compost in around six to nine months to mulch around five to six raised beds measuring 1m x 3m (3 x 10ft) annually. With a bin any smaller, you will be waiting much longer for finished compost, but regular turning of the material can speed up this process. Good airflow is also for decomposition and preventing smelly compost, so a bin made from wooden slats, pallets, or posts and wire is a good choice.

BIN TYPES

Pallet bin
Simply screw four upended pallets together to create a box frame and start filling with material. Once it has decomposed, unscrew one of the pallets for access.

Slot-together bin
Bought as a kit, this type of bin looks smart and is easy to assemble (pictured p37). Simply remove the slats to access finished compost.

Wire bin
Staple chicken wire to a frame consisting of four fence posts to make an extremely low-cost option. Have one end open both for filling and then easy access to the finished compost.

Stick bin
With a good local supply of willow or hazel, you can create a beautiful woven bin around a frame of eight or nine thick stakes hammered into the ground. Access to compost is only possible from the top.

Pathway composting
Line the pathway between two beds with cardboard, add a layer of woodchip, then pile waste material on top. Turn the material regularly with a fork and keep walking on it to speed up decomposition.

Simple mound
You can make compost without a structure if you have the space. Simply pile material up into a large mound but set aside time for regular turning and "re-mounding".

FILLING THE BIN: GREENS AND BROWNS

Two types of ingredients are used for composting – green (high in nitrogen) and brown (high in carbon). For every bucket of green material you add to a compost bin, always add a bucket of brown material. Too much green will result in slimy (anaerobic) compost; too much brown will seriously slow down decomposition. A volume ratio of 50:50 is ideal.

Tip
Covering the base of your bin with a 5–7cm (2–2¾in) layer of twigs and branches can help provide good airflow and improve decomposition rates.

Green materials

> Used coffee grounds and plastic-free tea bags

> Weeds (no seedheads)

> Grass clippings (unsprayed)

> Fruit and vegetable scraps

> Horse, cow, rabbit, and chicken manure

> Freshly cut plant material

> Seaweed (leave out in the rain before adding to wash off excess salt)

> Spent brewery grain (from a local brewery)

> Hair clippings (from barbers/hairdressers)

> Wool (from packaging)

Brown materials

> Cardboard and newspaper

> Dust from vacuuming

> Chippings and sawdust (from untreated wood)

> Autumn leaves (ideally shredded by lawnmower)

> Hay and straw

> Autumn and winter woody prunings

> Fallen pine needles

> Wood ash

> Tissues and paper towels

> Spent compost (from this season's pots)

When the bin is full
Once you have finished filling your bin, empty 4–5 cans of water over the contents then place a layer of cardboard on top and weigh it down with stones or bricks to keep off excess rain. Too much water can delay decomposition.

To speed up the composting process, turn the pile every six to eight weeks to incorporate air and move less-decomposed outer material inwards into the core. Compost piles shrink as organic materials decompose, so don't be surprised if yours ends up half its original size.

Finished compost
Compost is ready when the majority of the material is dark in colour and virtually unrecognizable. It is often full of earthworms (pictured opposite, below) and other beneficial organisms and the texture should be crumbly with a lovely earthy-fresh smell. Large pieces that haven't fully broken down can easily be removed and added to the next compost bin.

Three rules for making good compost

> The wider the variety of ingredients you add, the greater the range of nutrients in the finished compost.

> The smaller you chop up the greens and brown material, the faster it will break down.

> Keep at it. There's no such thing as too much homemade compost.

Composting Resources

Sourcing materials for making compost couldn't be easier. Although farmyard manure is easier to come by in the countryside, urban areas are a great source of cardboard and coffee grounds, as well as pallets for making the bin itself.

Vegetable scraps
Some of the most valuable composting ingredients out there, uncooked vegetable scraps and peelings all too often go to waste (pictured right). Approach your friends, neighbours, and local cafés, then set up a regular collection for a supply of nutrient-rich material.

Coffee grounds
Collect this underrated composting material from local cafés and regularly add them to your heap. Coffee grounds are not only high in nitrogen, but also contain good amounts of nutrients, such as potassium, that improve yields. You can also spread a 2–3cm (¾–1¼in) layer

around mature crops such as stemmed brassicas, as well as around soft fruit and Jerusalem artichokes.

Cardboard
Provided that the surface isn't glossy or covered with plastic tape, plain cardboard is one of the best sources of carbon. This is the brown material needed to balance nitrogen-rich greens when making compost (see p36). It also makes an excellent weed-suppressing cover for bare ground over winter, and a thick layer will stop your compost pile getting too wet, which slows down decomposition. Source supplies from local shops and businesses.

Grass clippings
Widespread in suburban areas, lawns are a great source of nitrogen-rich grass clippings. Collect them from neighbours who don't use fertilizers or sprays, then add to your compost heap in shallow 3cm (1¼ in) layers. Also spread clippings around crops, such as tomatoes, to lock in moisture and feed the soil as they break down.

Woodchip
I find woodchip an excellent material for surfacing paths. It's soft underfoot, soaks up rain and stops grass paths getting muddy. Remove the partly decomposed woodchip every two years and add it to the compost bin. You can often source

replacement woodchip for free from tree surgeons working in your local area.

Seaweed
After storms in coastal areas, collect collect a couple of small bags of seaweed and place straight onto your heap (check local laws first). You can also spread seaweed on raised beds over winter as a mulch, or make it into a plant feed.

Wool
This slow-release nitrogen-rich material can be added to the compost bin. It can also be spread around young plants to protect them from slug damage, suppress weeds, and retain moisture. Approach local farmers and pay or barter before you source wool.

Farmyard manure
With ready access to horse manure mixed with straw bedding, you have everything you need to fill a hot bed. Horse, cow, and poultry manure are all excellent green materials for adding to the compost heap.

Pallets
Often dumped in landfill, pallets can be used for a variety of simple DIY construction projects. With just a basic toolkit you can turn them into compost bins, planters, hot-bed outer frames, and use the individual planks to aid seed germination (see p31).

The Growing Year

Monthly Sowing and Growing Plans

Starting in March, I've divided the self-sufficiency garden's growing season into months, up to and including October. November and the winter months are combined into one section, then the growing year starts afresh in spring with the second season. Each month features a plan of the whole garden with a key indicating what is already growing or needs planting out in the different areas. Each area is then covered in detail, starting with the polytunnel where seeds are sown.

GARDEN LAYOUT

The plan of the self-sufficiency garden, which is the size of a half-allotment plot (125 sq m/150 sq yds), is shown opposite. On it are marked the different areas of the garden including the polytunnel with its beds, seedling shelves, and propagation and tool bench. The outside growing area consists of two hot beds, three hoop beds, six main raised beds, a keyhole bed for salads, and the herb and edible flower bed. In addition, I grow soft fruit and some veg in the borders around the perimeter, and I also keep a "spares" bed for any leftover seedlings. Potatoes grow in pots and I even manage to squeeze a squash or two in the compost bin!

For each month of the growing season you'll see exactly the same plan of the garden. The various growing areas feature black "pins" with numbers corresponding to the particular crop planted there. Some crops will remain in their beds for four months or more; others for less. When a crop is harvested and cleared over the course of the month, the replacement crop is denoted by a grey pin on the plan.

Alongside each plan, a key lists the numbers on the plan and their corresponding crops, grouped by growing area.

Following the plan and key, I cover in detail what is happening in each of the garden's growing areas in the same order every month, making it easier to keep track of what has been sown, planted out, and harvested in the garden.

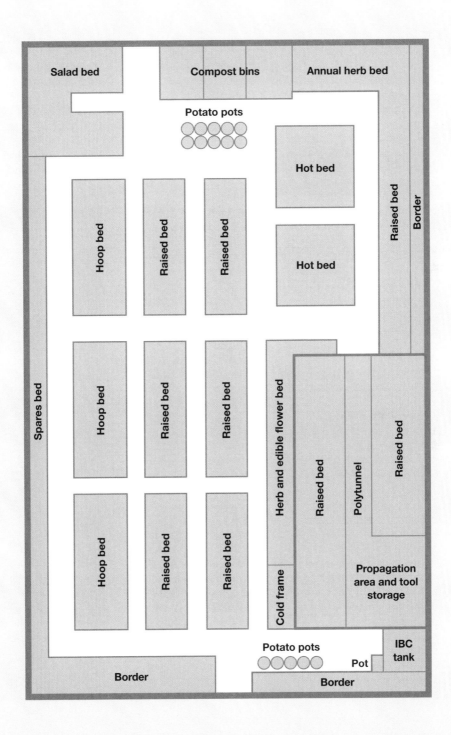

SOWING

In almost every month of the growing season, I start off seeds in module trays. This sowing information can be found under Polytunnel, and is presented in chart form. Each crop is listed with the monthly sowing time, size of module cell used, how many seeds to sow per cell, sowing depth, cell count, and finally how many seeds to thin to.

Cell sizes

In terms of module cell sizes, the one I use most is 4cm (1½in), but there are two other useful sizes. Each offers a specific benefit in relation to the crop you are sowing or growing in it.

Deep: With a depth of 10–12cm (4–4¾in), these module trays are ideal for sowing fava or runner beans, both of which have deep roots.

Standard: (4cm/1½in diameter) This is the standard cell size and will work for the majority of crops. It allows seedlings enough space to grow and develop strongly without becoming stressed.

Large: (7cm/2¾in diameter) This is ideal for tomato and squash seedlings to allow them to develop a few

mature leaves and a strong root system before you transplant them.

Quantities

On each chart, I recommend how many modules to sow and how many seeds per cell under "cell count" and "seeds per cell". The seed quantities given are on the generous side to allow for losses through poor germination, or owing to slug damage after transplanting. Hold on to any spare seedlings for at least two weeks to plug any gaps, then find them a new home.

Timings

Every single growing season is different and it's vital to understand that gardening is at the mercy of Mother Nature. An unexpected late frost may arrive, or the month may be much wetter or drier than average, and gardeners must work with that. The timings of when to sow in that particular month, as well as when to harvest are, therefore, as accurate as I could make them. They are based on my experience of what happened over one growing season in the self-sufficiency garden and I offer them as a guide. Conditions may vary a little in your particular location, but you will still enjoy a delicious harvest, even if sometimes a crop will take

a little longer to mature. On the other hand, it may be ready in record time.

SQUARE-METRE GARDENING

Over a single growing season, every harvest from

the self-sufficiency garden was weighed and duly noted down. The results not only blew my original goal out of the water, but provided a huge amount of valuable data. As a result, I have been able to create a square-metre gardening guide (see pp142–145) that calculates expected yields per square metre (10 square feet) for all the main crops, alongside plant quantities and average yield per plant. I hope, going forward, that it will help you organize your own space for maximum productivity.

On the following pages you will find the breakdown of the total yield from the self-sufficiency garden in its first year. Then in March, the new growing season begins.

First Season Harvests

During the growing season, it can be difficult to appreciate how much food your garden produces. Consistent harvests quickly build up, and I was stunned to see just how much food a garden can produce over a season. In this chart, I'm sharing all the harvests from the first year of the self-sufficiency garden. In the end, we exceeded expectations and grew almost 600kg (1,325 lb) of produce! I recommend you keep a rough track of the food you harvest: all you need is a simple set of scales by the garden gate and a notepad. You too will be surprised just how much it is possible to grow.

SELLING SURPLUS

When your garden produces more food than your family can eat or preserve, it's the perfect opportunity to sell your surplus. But before you start, check out your local council regulations on selling homegrown produce. When selling, I recommend offering a "pay what you feel" or "donations" approach. My sales from this year's surplus have covered the cost of my seed order, which is another self-sufficiency achievement.

The more surplus produce you sell, the more you can invest in your garden.

EXTRA HARVESTS

In addition to the main harvests listed opposite, many of the crops grown in the self-sufficiency garden produce what I see as bonus harvests. These "extras" include coriander seeds, chive flowers, and dried climbing-bean seeds. They alone amounted to a total of 15kg (almost 34lb) of food.

Crop	Kilogram (to the nearest 100g)	Crop	Kilogram (to the nearest 100g)
Aubergine	4.3	Perpetual spinach	2.8
Beetroot	30.2	Potatoes	21.3
Carrots	22.3	Potatoes, container	19.3
Cauliflower	7.3	Potatoes, new	16.2
Celery (crop failure)	0.8	Purple sprouting broccoli	3.4
Chard	6.6	Radish	4.3
Chilli	0.3	Radish, daikon	15.3
Climbing beans	19.3	Radish, winter	4.1
Courgette (including marrows)	32.4	Rhubarb	7.9
Cucumber (indoor)	28.7	Salad (salad bed and hot bed)	12.9
Cucumber (outdoor)	17.1	Shallots	2.4
Dwarf beans	2.4	Spring onion	1.9
Fennel	8.6	Swede	12.8
Field beans	4.2	Tomatoes	74.1
Garlic	3.3	Tree cabage	6.7
Jerusalem artichokes	29.5	Turnip	3.8
Kale	2.8	Winter cabbage	14.4
Kohlrabi	5.9	Winter squash	32.3
Leek	16.6		
Napa cabbage	10.9	**Extras**	15
Onions	28.4	Berries	1.9
Pak choi	9	Herbs, annual	1.7
Parsnips	10.9	Herbs, perennial	0.7
Peas	9	**Grand total**	586

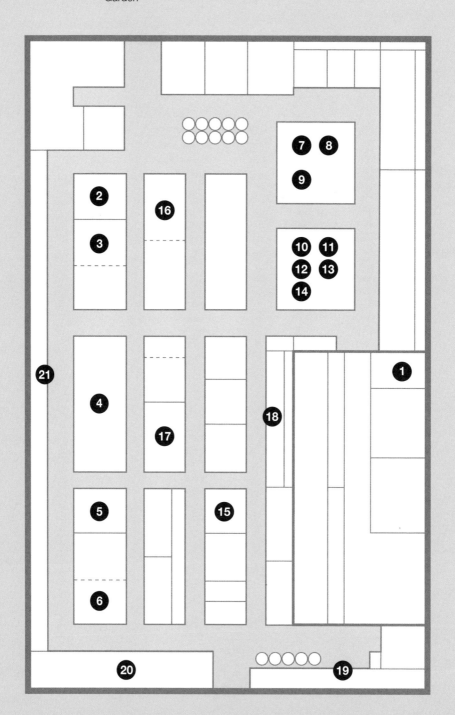

March

March may feel like the start of spring but for most, there are many frosts ahead, so be patient. Getting the hot beds up and running is the priority. Your first crops from them should be ready to harvest in as little as four weeks, and the beds will go on to produce a huge amount of food during May, June, and beyond. In the polytunnel, under cover sowing in modules starts in earnest in March. The first half of the month is also your final opportunity to plant out new perennials so they settle in well. Also, if you are creating a new garden, aim to finish any projects this month. Things will get really busy in April.

Key:

Polytunnel
1. Coriander

Hoop beds
2. New potatoes
3. Pak choi
4. Potatoes
5. Beetroot
6. Cauliflower

Hot bed 1
7. Carrots
8. Spring onions
9. Turnips

Hot bed 2
10. Peas (for shoots)
11. Lettuce
12. Spinach
13. Radish
14. Pak choi

Raised beds
15. Garlic
16. Field beans
17. New potatoes

Herb and edible flower bed
18. Perennial herbs

Borders
19. Jerusalem artichokes
20. Soft fruit
21. Spares bed

IN THE POLYTUNNEL

Beds

These won't be filled until it's warm enough to transplant the summer crops, such as tomatoes and cucumbers, in May. Take advantage of the space to **sow** some coriander seed direct to start harvesting leaves in May and June.

On the seedling shelves

Start off several crops in pots and modules this month to fill up the garden as quickly as you can, and ensure it's packed with produce for as long as possible. Make additional shelving space by inserting four posts into one of the polytunnel beds and balancing a pallet or sheet of wood on top.

Courgettes

For early crops, **sow** 1 courgette seed 0.5cm (¼in) deep in each of 3 x 7cm (2¾in) pots and half-bury these pots, between two rows of crops in one of the hot beds. The bottom-heat will kick start germination and you'll get healthy courgette seedlings.

Tomatoes

Start off tomatoes – one of the most important crops of the year – in March, again utilizing the bottom heat produced by the hot bed. I recommend sowing your tomato seeds, including tumbling types, in narrow seed trays with a 5cm (2in) layer of compost added to the base. **Cover** with 1cm (½in) of compost and **water** lightly. Insert labels (I make mine from yoghurt pots cut into strips) to separate the different varieties, then **place** on one of the hot beds in between two rows of seeds you've already sown. Narrow seed trays won't block the light from the seedlings emerging in these rows.

When the first true leaves appear, carefully **prick out** the tomato seedlings and transplant up to the base of the first leaves in individual

Crop	Sowing week	Cell type	Seeds per cell	Sowing depth	Cell count	Thin to
Beetroot	1	4cm (1½in)	4–5	2cm (¾in)	20	3–4
Cauliflower	1	7cm (2¾in)	2	2cm (¾in)	6	1
Field beans	1	Deep	1	5cm (2in)	40	N/A
Pak choi	1	4cm (1½in)	2	1cm (½in)	20	1
Onion (sets)	2	4cm (1½in)	1	cover 2/3 of set	120	1
Napa cabbage	2	4cm (1½in)	2	1cm (½in)	12	1
Perpetual spinach	2	4cm (1½in)	2	2cm (¾in)	8	1
Dwarf bean	3	7cm (2¾in)	1	3–4cm (1–1½in)	10	N/A
Radish	3	4cm (1½in)	3–4	2cm (¾in)	8	N/A
Peas	4	4cm (1½in)	3	2–3cm (¾–1¼in)	30	N/A

7cm (2¾ in) pots. Make sure you label every pot, and then place these back on the hot bed, half buried. On particularly cold nights, **cover** the growing frame and lights with an old carpet or thick blanket to protect the tender seedlings.

Aubergines and chillies

To grow these crops from seed, you really need to start them off in February. Do this next season, following the same sowing technique as for tomatoes and then utilizing the heat of the hot beds (see left). But if you do want to get a harvest from aubergines and chillies this year, see May (p67), then I advise purchasing young plants from a garden centre.

HOOP BEDS

Water during warm spring weather: these covered raised beds can quickly dry out. **Uncover** during the daytime for ventilation to maintain good airflow around the crops.

Potatoes

In the first week of March, the new potatoes go in. Aim to **plant** 12 seed potatoes 20cm (8in) deep in a 4 x 3 grid to take up a third of one of the hoop beds. Later, in mid-March, **plant** the entire middle hoop bed with your chosen variety of potato. I love growing 'Charlotte' owing to consistent yields and excellent flavour. Plant chitted seed potatoes 20cm

(8in) deep and spaced more widely at 35–40cm (12–18in) intervals. Make diagonal rows, 30cm (12in) apart.

Transplant pak choi, beetroot, and cauliflower seedlings (pictured above, right), which may be small, into the hoop beds by the end of the month. They won't need hardening off as they will still be under cover. **Space** the pak choi seedlings 15cm (6in) apart, in diagonal rows 10cm (4in) apart, and use the same spacing for the clumps of beetroot seedlings. Cauliflower seedlings will grow much larger so **plant** 4 in a square, each 50cm (20in) apart, with a fifth cauliflower in the middle.

HOT BEDS

March is still winter for most gardens in the UK, and it's important to keep the lights in place on your hot beds unless it's a particularly warm day. However, as long as the outside temperature is above freezing, you can **wedge open** for 10–15 minutes in the morning. This will allow for good ventilation and benefit the tender seedlings, such as tomatoes, which will be started off in these beds.

Bed 1
Fill the bed (see p20) in the first week of March to a depth of around 70cm (28in) to retain heat until at least late May. Two days after filling the bed, **sow** carrots in rows 1, 3, 5, and 7; onions go in rows 2 and 6; and turnips in row 5. Sow all these seeds at a depth of 2cm (¾in).

Bed 2
Fill this bed to a depth of around 60cm (24in) in the second week of March to retain heat until at least early May. Once filled, **leave** for two days to settle and then **sow** lettuce in rows 1 and 7; radish in rows 2 and 6; spinach in row 3; peas for shoots in row 4 (pictured below); and pak choi in row 5. All seeds can be sown 1cm (½in) deep with the exception of peas, which need a depth of 2–3cm (¾–1¼in). The seeds will germinate quickly in the heat of the beds.

RAISED BEDS

March is still early for planting most crops in the raised beds but new potatoes, garlic, and field beans can go in.

Plant out new potatoes in mid-March in a 5 x 3 grid to occupy half a bed (5 seed potatoes lengthways), and at a depth of 20cm (8in).

Field bean seedlings should be ready to **plant out** around the last week of March. **Harden off** the plants in the cold frame over a 2–3 day period before spacing them at 20cm (8in) intervals in staggered rows 20cm (8in) apart. There should be enough space for around 30 field bean plants, or

approximately 4 long rows of 7–8 plants each.

Although garlic is best planted in autumn, early spring-planted varieties are available. A 1m (3ft) square area of the bed should be enough space for about 100 cloves. **Plant** each clove at a depth of 5cm (2in). Allow 10cm (4in) between each clove, and in staggered rows 10cm (4in) apart.

SALAD BED

Leave this space empty but keep on top of any weeds.

HERBS

Annuals
Nothing to do in March.

Perennials
Transplant all perennial herbs into their permanent locations by the end of the month. Sourcing cuttings from family and friends, such as rosemary (pictured above) and thyme, as well as divisions from established herbs, such as mint and chives, is a great, low-cost way to establish your own herb collection. Unlike annual vegetables, these herbs don't need a handful of compost at the base of the hole. **Water** each plant or division generously, straight after transplanting. There are also many fantastic online herb retailers offering rare and exciting varieties to grow.

EDIBLE FLOWERS

If you plan to grow violas, **put** the seeds in the fridge at the start of March. A period of cold will speed up germination when you sow them next month.

BORDERS

Most of the perennials in the borders were chosen as additions to the main crops we grow for self-sufficiency. To supplement your own planting, **choose** perennials that really excite you. I love roses, and they offer not only beauty and fragrance, but also edible flowers and hips. You may, for example, want to **grow** a magnolia instead of a rose, include a dwarf apple

tree, or maybe plant globe artichokes.

Jerusalem artichokes

These tubers (pictured opposite) need to be planted by mid-March. **Dig** a hole around 20cm (8in) deep and **add** a generous handful of compost or vegetable scraps at the base. Next, **place** a tuber on its side in the hole and backfill. Repeat, spacing the tubers at 30cm (12in) intervals until you've planted a row of 12–14 tubers, then plant a second row in a staggered pattern 25cm (10in) away from the first. You should expect to harvest around 15–30kg (33–66lb) of delicious tubers throughout the winter.

Soft fruit

We wanted currants, berries, and rhubarb in the borders to supplement the main food crops and add sweetness to meals. If you also plan to include fruit, **plant out** currant bushes and rhubarb crowns (pictured above) this month. Young strawberry plants can also be set out in the borders now.

Spares bed

I have one raised bed in the borders that I set aside as space for transplanting any spare seedlings over the growing year. A spare bed is also really useful if you forget to sow a particular crop, or you see something you would love to try but the rest of the growing space is already occupied.

COMPOST

Get into the habit of keeping a container in the kitchen to **collect** veg scraps and other materials (see p38) so you can start to fill up your first compost bin as soon as possible. March, before the growing season kicks in, is also a good time to **explore** sources of additional compost ingredients in your local community. For example, I collect used coffee grounds from three to four cafés on a weekly basis.

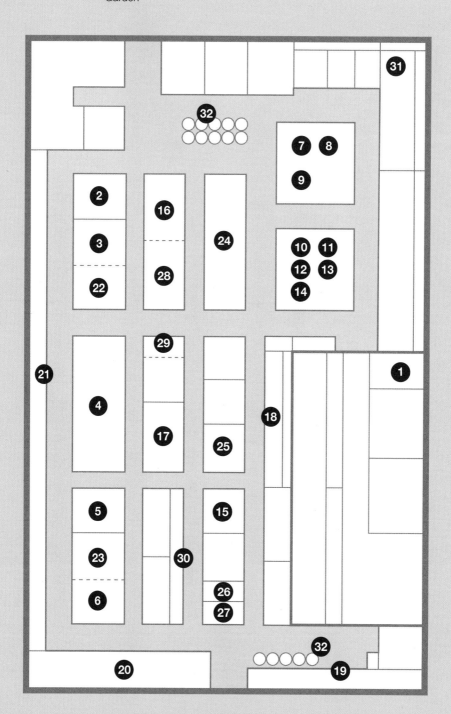

April

April brings the excitement of your first harvests from this year's sowings, with radish, pea shoots, lettuce, and spinach all ready in the second hot bed. There's plenty of sowing to be done this month too, so why not team up with other local gardeners to bulk-buy good quality multipurpose compost? It will be much cheaper than buying single bags from the local garden centre and create less plastic waste. And given April will be busy, it's a good idea to set aside an hour or so each weekend to make a checklist for the coming week. You'll get the important jobs done, and tick off all those small tasks that, added together, can make a big difference.

Key:

Polytunnel
1. Coriander

Hoop beds
2. New potatoes
3. Pak choi
22. Courgettes
4. Potatoes
5. Beetroot
23. Dwarf beans
6. Cauliflower

Hot bed 1
7. Carrots
8. Spring onions
9. Turnips

Hot bed 2
10. Peas (for shoots)
11. Lettuce
12. Spinach
13. Radish
14. Pak choi

Raised beds
16. Field beans
28. Napa cabbage
29. Leeks
17. New potatoes
30. Peas
24. Onions
25. Parsnips
15. Garlic
26. Perpetual spinach
27. Radish
31. Shallots

Herb and edible flower bed
18. Perennial herbs

Borders
19. Jerusalem artichokes
20. Soft fruit
21. Spares bed
32. Potato pots

IN THE POLYTUNNEL

Beds

Water regularly, taking care to not overwater coriander seedlings (left). A good rule of thumb is to water when the top 2–3cm (1in) of soil/compost feels dry. And it's important to keep on top of weeds, which will now be on the increase.

ON THE SEEDLING SHELVES

Peas, dwarf beans, onions, radish (pictured below), and perpetual spinach sown last month will be developing

Crop	Sowing week	Cell type	Seeds per cell	Sowing depth	Cell count	Thin to
Kohlrabi	1	4cm (1½ in)	2	2cm (¾in)	20	N/A
Beetroot	2	4cm (1½ in)	4–5	2cm (¾in)	40	3–4
Fennel	2	4cm (1½ in)	2	2cm (¾in)	20	1
Peas	2	4cm (1½ in)	3	2-3cm (¾–1in)	80	3
Tree cabbage	2	7cm (2¾ in)	2	2cm (¾in)	8	1
Cucumber	3	7cm (2¾ in)	1	1cm (½in)	8	N/A
Turnip	3	4cm (1½ in)	3–4	2cm (¾in)	20	3

nicely, so **check** moisture levels regularly.

Start off vegetables in modules. Check the table (left) for what to sow, when to sow, and at what depth.

Celery

Sow under cover because celery can be tricky to germinate and needs extra warmth. Fill a seed tray with 6–7cm (2½–2¾in) of compost and gently scatter celery seeds on the surface leaving around 2–3cm (¾–1in) between each seed. Gently press the seeds into the compost and then mist with water; no need to cover. Enclose the tray in a clear plastic bag to create a mini-greenhouse and place on a warm windowsill indoors. Once the seedlings have appeared, remove the bag and keep them watered.

HOOP BEDS

Transplant courgettes that germinated in the hot bed in March, spacing the two strongest plants 75cm (30in) apart and 30cm (12in) from the end of the bed with the new potatoes and pak choi. From June, when the hoop beds are mostly uncovered, these two plants can spread over onto the path, rather than impacting the other crops in the bed. At the end of the month, **transplant** dwarf beans in between the beetroot and cauliflower,

spacing them fairly close together at just 12–15cm (4¾–6in) apart and in blocks so the stems support each other as they grow. Protect courgettes and dwarf beans, which are both tender. Keep an eye on the weather and **take action** (see pp212–213) if a cold snap is forecast.

HOT BEDS

Bed 1

Boosted by the heat of the bed, carrots, onions, and turnips will be putting on a lot of growth. Keep a close eye on the moisture levels from the second week of April and **water** when necessary. **Harvest** the first turnips if you like to eat them fairly small.

Bed 2

After picking your first radish, **move** the pots of tomato seedlings into the space they have freed up. You can bury a plank 5cm (2in) deep into the hot bed and place the pots on top of it to avoid the tomato roots growing into the surrounding compost. Pea shoots, lettuce, and spinach are now ready to **harvest** and turn into your first homegrown salad of the season. Water the plants when needed, and **ventilate** by propping the lights open on warm days. When the tomatoes start getting too large for the hot bed growing frame, **move** them in their

pots to a sunny windowsill indoors (the polytunnel will still be too cold).

RAISED BEDS

In April, the raised beds slowly come to life and it's exciting to see the first garlic shoots emerge. Regularly **weed** the beds (and the rest of the garden), making it part of your weekly routine so April's strong weed growth doesn't get out of hand.

Parsnips

Sow parsnips direct because they don't transplant well owing to their fragile taproots. Make rows 2cm (¾in) deep, 15cm (6in) apart, and **sow** parsnip seeds thinly (1 seed every 2cm/¾in) before covering over and watering well. The seedlings take a while to appear so be patient. And don't let the soil dry out as this will severely impact germination. Use the plank method to improve success rates (see p31) and once seedlings appear, **thin** to 1 every 10cm (4in).

Onions

Transplant the onion sets from the seedling shelves once the leaves are around 10cm (4in) tall. Space each set 15cm (6in) apart and plant in staggered rows 10cm (4in) apart. Onions don't need hardening off.

Peas

First **make** a structure for the peas to climb up, depending on how tall that variety will grow. Then **plant out** the clumps of peas 5cm (2in) apart once the seedlings have reached a height of 6–7cm (2½–2¾in). I grow 'Oregon Sugar Pod', which reaches just 1m (3ft), and make a simple trellis from sticks and string.

Radish

Transplant the clumps of radish seedlings from the seedling shelves, spacing them 10cm (4in) apart and in staggered rows 10cm (4in) apart.

Perpetual spinach

When they have a few true leaves, **plant out** the spinach in 2 rows. Allow 20cm (8in) between each plant so they can put on a lot of growth and supply you with abundant delicious leaves.

Leeks

I prefer to **start off** leeks in a seed bed, not in modules, then transplant to their final location – the space left by clearing the napa cabbage and field beans in July. Because leeks are slow to mature, sow in the first or second week of April. Use the handle of a rake to create two rows 2cm (¾in) deep, 15cm (6in) apart, and **sow** the seeds thickly (1–2 seeds every 1cm/½in). Then cover back over, label, and keep them well watered.

Shallots

As with onions, I grow shallots from sets. **Plant out** sets directly where they are to grow in the first half of April, burying two-thirds of each set. Allow 10cm (4in) between each set and plant out in staggered rows 10cm (4in) apart.

Napa cabbage

Transplant the napa cabbage next to the field beans (pictured opposite).

Space plants 35cm (14in) apart in rows that are 35cm (14in) apart.

SALAD BED

Nothing to do in April.

HERBS

Annuals

In mid-April, **sow** annual herbs in modules (basil is pictured below), starting with the four listed below. You could then add chervil and summer savory; both are sown and thinned as for dill.

Perennials

Now the perennial herbs are settling into their homes you'll see a huge amount of growth. If you transplanted a clump of chives in March, start to **harvest** a few leaves this month to add to salads.

Crop	Sowing week	Cell Type	Seeds per cell	Sowing depth	Cell count	Thin to
Basil	2	4cm (1½in)	5–6	1cm (½in)	40	3
Coriander*	2	4cm (1½in)	5–6	2cm (¾in)	20	4
Dill*	2	4cm (1½in)	4–5	1cm (½in)	10	3
Parsley*	2	4cm (1½in)	4–5	2cm (¾in)	10	3

*To save space, these three herbs can be sown in the same 40-cell module tray.

EDIBLE FLOWERS

Crop	Sowing week	Cell type	Seeds per cell	Sowing depth	Cell count	Thin to
Borage	3	7cm (2¾in)	2	1cm (½in)	5	1
Calendula*	2	4cm (1½in)	2	2cm (¾in)	20	1
Cornflower*	2	4cm (1½in)	4–5	1cm (½in)	10	3
Edible viola*	2	4cm (1½in)	2–3	1cm (½in)	10	1
Nasturtium	2	7cm (2¾in)	1	3cm (1¼in)	6	N/A

*To save space, these three flowers can be sown in the same 40-cell module tray.

Sow my top five edible flowers under cover this month. Nasturtium, borage, and calendula seeds are easy to save in autumn, so you won't need to buy these flower seeds ever again. And if self-seeders pop up in random spots, gently **uproot** with a trowel and **transplant** them to another loation.

BORDERS

Potato pots
Potatoes are an excellent crop for container growing and a few large pots will supplement harvests from the beds. I choose a maincrop variety that will take most of the season to mature, then stack the pots when the plants die back in autumn. My go-to variety is 'Sarpo Mira' because of its excellent blight resistance. Over winter, store the pots in a polytunnel or garden shed, and tip out the contents of one pot at a time whenever you need to harvest spuds; no storing is necessary!

Plant up containers holding 30–35 litres (6½ gallons). These are the best size and light enough to carry around the garden. Fill with 50 per cent soil, leaf mould, or spent compost mixed with 50 per cent compost or well-rotted manure. If you are short on compost, mix in up to 20 per cent shredded autumn leaves, seaweed, or grass clippings. Plant two seed potatoes just above the halfway point, then cover with the compost mix, leaving a 2–3cm (¾–1¼in) gap below the rim of the pot for a mulch that will retain water. Grass clippings and woodchip both work well as mulches. Make sure you **water** the pot thoroughly after planting, using at least 5 litres (1 gallon) of water.

COMPOST

Keep adding material to your first compost bin throughout the month. If you can't generate enough from your own home and garden, consider sourcing additional supplies from friends, family, neighbours, and colleagues.

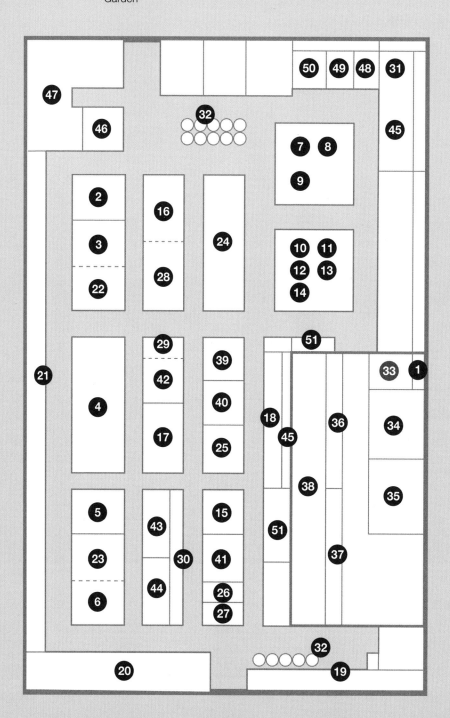

May

May, when the frosts are finally over, is my favourite month in the garden and a very dynamic time. Temperatures are rising, the days are noticeably longer, and there are numerous seedlings waiting to be planted out. The first big harvests from the hot beds are another cause for celebration. With the warming temperatures and the long daylight hours, crops will be growing rapidly, and as the garden greens up, you'll observe changes almost on a daily basis. But with so much growth on the plot, it's important to keep on top of any weeds. These will compete with young plants for both moisture and nutrients.

Key:

Polytunnel
1. Coriander
33. Coriander > **Chillies**
34. Aubergine
35. Cucumber
36. Basil
37. Tumbling tomatoes
38. Vine tomatoes

Hoop beds
2. New potatoes
3. Pak choi
22. Courgette
4. Potatoes
5. Beetroot
23. Dwarf beans
6. Cauliflower

Hot bed 1
7. Carrots
8. Spring onions
9. Turnips

Hot bed 2
10. Peas (for shoots)
11. Lettuce
12. Spinach
13. Radish
14. Pak choi

Raised beds
46. Celery
16. Field beans
28. Napa cabbage
29. Leeks
42. Tree cabbage
17. New potatoes
30. Peas
43. Beetroot
44. Fennel
24. Onions
39. Turnip
40. Swede
25. Parsnips
15. Garlic
41. Kohlrabi
26. Perpetual spinach
27. Radish
31. Shallots
45. Peas

Salad bed
47. Salad leaves

Herb and edible flower bed
51. Edible flowers
18. Perennial herbs
45. Peas
50. Coriander
49. Parsley
48. Dill

Borders
19. Jerusalem artichokes
20. Soft fruit
21. Spares bed
32. Potato pots

IN THE POLYTUNNEL

Beds
Tomatoes

From the second week of May, **transfer** the potted tomatoes from indoors to the polytunnel. Start with the vine tomatoes, and **transplant** them into the 6m (20ft) bed, which will accommodate 2 staggered rows of 9 or 10 plants, allowing 60cm (2ft) spacing between both the plants and the rows. This will ensure adequate light and airflow for each plant, reducing potential disease issues later in summer. For sturdy stems, plant them up to the first set of leaves, after making a deep hole and **add** two generous handfuls of compost to the base. **Water** thoroughly. After a few days, **set up** a simple trellis system to support the plants. First, loosely tie a length of heavy duty string around the base of the stem, then wrap it around the plant in a spiral, tying the top to a horizontal crop bar. Use a slip knot so you can slacken the string as the plant grows.

Transplant the potted tumbling tomatoes into the same bed, 30cm (12in) apart. Although they don't need to go in as deep as the vine types, **add** a generous handful or two of compost to the bottom of the hole. Support isn't necessary: they will sprawl over the side of the bed.

Basil

April-sown basil will be ready to **transplant** into the polytunnel by mid- to late May. I set the plants in a long row in one of the beds for ease of harvesting. Space clumps of seedlings 10cm (4in) apart and water in thoroughly. Alternatively, you can **underplant** the tomatoes with basil to serve as a living mulch.

Coriander and chilli
Remove most of the coriander plants at the end of the month but leave a few at the back to flower and produce seed to enjoy fresh or dried. At the start of May, **buy in** young chilli plants from your local garden centre then in mid-May **transplant** into the bed. Space them 40cm (16in) apart, then water in.

Aubergine
As with chillies, transplant bought-in aubergine plants (pictured left), spacing them 50cm (20in) apart. The fruits that form later will be heavy, so my go-to method is a 1.2m (4ft) wooden stake pushed 30cm (12in) into the soil. As it grows, loosely tie the stem to it with twine.

Cucumber
A pyramid trellis made with 4 x 1.6m (5ft) canes is my favourite **support** for cucumbers. There will be enough space for two pyramids, which are easy to set up as well as looking good. **Insert** the canes 60cm (2ft) apart, tie the tops together, and plant a seedling at the base of each cane. Consistent watering is key because irregular watering can lead to bitter-tasting cucumbers.

Mulch the base of the plants with grass clippings to ensure the soil stays moist so you'll get high yields. You can also train cucumbers vertically. Use the method mentioned for vine and cordon tomatoes (see June, p78).

ON THE SEEDLING SHELVES

As well as cucumber, you'll have celery, kohlrabi, beetroot, tree cabbage, turnip, fennel, and peas ready to **plant out** this month, conveniently making space for the next batch of sowings (see below).

Crop	Sowing week	Cell type	Seeds per cell	Sowing depth	Cell count	Thin to
Cauliflower	1	7cm (2¾in)	1	2cm (¾in)	8	1
Climbing beans	1	7cm (2¾in)	1	3–4cm (1¼–1½in)	40	N/A
Courgette	1	7cm (2¾in)	2	0.5cm (¼in)	6	1
Kohlrabi	1	4cm (1½in)	2	2cm (¾in)	20	1
Purple sprouting broccoli	1	4cm (1½in)	2	2cm (¾in)	8	1
Pumpkin	1	7cm (2¾in)	2	0.5cm (¼in)	2	1
Winter squash	1	7cm (2¾in)	2	0.5cm (¼in)	2	1
Cucumber	2	7cm (2¾in)	2	0.5cm (¼in)	6	1
Dwarf beans	2	4cm (1½in)	1	2cm (¾in)	20	N/A
Chard	3	4cm (1½in)	3–4	2cm (¾in)	20	3
Radish	3	4cm (1½in)	3–4	2cm (¾in)	40	N/A

HOOP BEDS

There isn't much to do in the hoop beds except **water** the potatoes (pictured opposite), **weed**, **ventilate**, and begin to **harvest** the pak choi (pictured opposite, below left). You can **feed** all the crops with homemade liquid fertilizer (see p210) every two weeks to boost growth and health.

HOT BEDS

May is an exciting month, with harvests coming thick and fast from both hot beds. Those based on horse manure or seaweed won't need any additional feed, but for those made with ramial chipped wood, I recommend **applying** a homemade liquid feed every fortnight.

Bed 1

By the second half of the month you'll be enjoying fresh turnips, plus small carrots and very young spring onions – these last two harvested primarily from thinning the rows. **Pick** the biggest first, allowing the smaller ones to grow on so you can harvest into July.

Bed 2

Enjoy large harvests this month. Where radish, then tomato seedlings, were, **direct sow** another batch of radish to pick in early June. When **harvesting** spinach and lettuce (pictured below), always **remove** the outer leaves rather than cut whole plants. This creates space and keeps the plants cropping steadily over the next few weeks.

RAISED BEDS

Swede

Direct sow 1 seed every 2cm (¾in) in trenches 2cm (¾in) deep, leaving 15–20cm (6–8in) between rows. When true leaves appear, thin to 1 seedling every 10cm (4in) for large roots in winter.

Turnip

Transplant the turnip seedlings into the bed the first week of May. Allow 15cm (6in) between clumps and plant in staggered rows 10cm (4in) apart. You could also **sow direct** in rows 15cm (6in) apart.

Kohlrabi

Seedlings will be small but good enough to **transplant** by the end of the month. Plant out at 15cm (6in)

intervals, in staggered rows 15cm (6in) apart.

Tree cabbage

When they have 4-5 true leaves, **transplant** the first 4 seedlings. Pot on the other 2 to continue maturing until you remove the leek seedlings in July, and plant them in the freed-up space. The goal is to have 2 rows of 3 tree cabbage seedlings spaced 40cm (16in) apart, with 60cm (2ft) between each row.

Beetroot

Plant out the beetroot clumps in the first half of the month, allowing a 20cm (8in) space between each in staggered rows 15cm (6in) apart (pictured above).

Fennel

Harden off fennel seedlings then **plant out** around mid-month. Space each seedling 15–20cm (6–8in) apart in 3 staggered rows, 15cm (6in) apart.

Peas

You can never have too many peas! In addition to those transplanted in April (pictured opposite, top and bottom), **plant out** more, with supports, next to the shallots. Then tie string round the supports as they grow. **Space** the clumps of seedlings 7.5cm (3in) apart in staggered rows 7.5cm (3in) apart. Any spare pea seedlings can be **planted out** between the perennial herbs and the polytunnel.

Celery

Once the seedlings on your windowsill are 5cm (2in) tall, **pot on** each into a 7cm (2¾in) container and transfer them to the polytunnel shelves. **Transplant** at the end of the month, once the risk of frost has passed, with 30cm (12in) spacing between and in staggered rows 30cm (12in) apart.

Radish

Whenever you harvest radish from the small strip you've established, **fill** the gaps and ensure a steady supply by transplanting 10 clumps of seedlings every couple of weeks. For an alternative harvest, allow some plants to flower and set seed so you can add the flowers

to salads and eat the crunchy, green seed pods.

Garlic

If you've grown a hardneck variety of garlic, you will be able to enjoy delicious garlic scapes (flower stems, pictured above) in May and early June. Snap them off and lightly pan fry for fantastic flavour. Removing them also helps the plant concentrate its energy on bulb production rather than on flowering

SALAD BED

By the second week of May, the wait is finally over and it's time to **sow** salads. But before you get going, let me give you one piece of advice: choose the types of salad you most enjoy eating. I adore rocket and oriental greens but if you aren't a fan, don't grow them.

The large salad bed is designed for successional sowing, which means you'll get continuous crops. **Sow** only a third of the bed at a time, wait a couple of weeks before sowing the next third, and another couple before sowing the final third. Salad leaves can quickly become bitter during summer's hot and dry spells, but fortnightly sowings should produce enough fresh leaves to last until October. Sow seeds in shallow rows 1-2cm (½–¾in) deep, 15cm (6in) apart and keep the ground moist, especially until germination has taken place.

Salad crops

- Cima di rapa
- Chicory
- Field beans (tops)
- Komatsuna
- Lettuce (cos, gem, butterhead)
- Mizuna
- Mustard greens
- Peas (shoots)
- Rocket
- Sorrel
- Spinach
- Tatsoi

HERBS

Annuals
Dill, parsley, and coriander
Once these seedlings have 3–4 true leaves, **transplant** them into the borders. Parsley can be grown in a block with 15cm (6in) between each plant and row. Plant dill and coriander more closely, allowing 10cm (4in) between each clump of seedlings in staggered rows 8cm (3in) apart.

Perennials
Mint
May brings the first harvest from the March-transplanted mint. When you **pick** the tips from mint, leave at least 5cm (2in) of stem so the plant can send up new shoots.

Chives
With the plants in full production, **snip off** stems as you need them. In late May, beautiful purple flowers (pictured right) may appear: they are edible but always leave some for the bees.

EDIBLE FLOWERS

The second half of May is the perfect time to **plant out** the April-sown edible flowers in patches. Aim to plant tall borage at the back, sprawling nasturtiums at the edge of the bed, then **fill in** with calendula, viola, and cornflower seedlings spaced at 10cm (4in) intervals. You could also add interest and some more edibles by **interplanting** a few clumps of coriander or radish, then allow these clumps to flower and set seed.

BORDERS

For a splash of colour in the borders, I like to plant out sweet peas, as well as cosmos, that I've grown from seed.

Potato containers
Leafy growth will now appear, so ensure you **water** the plants well this month. For added colour but without impacting the potato crop, **plant** a nasturtium seedling in a couple of the pots to trail over the edge.

Soft fruit
Currants and berries will be flowering this month. To aid the development of fruits, keep the stems clear of weeds, then, after watering, **mulch** around them by putting down a layer of cardboard. Cover this with woodchip to keep the weeds down for the rest of the growing season.

COMPOST

Aim to **fill up** the first compost bin by the end of the month. If you need additional waste materials, **source** them from friends, family, and your local community. With a full bin, you will have a precious asset lined up for your next growing season.

The
**Self-
Sufficiency**
Garden

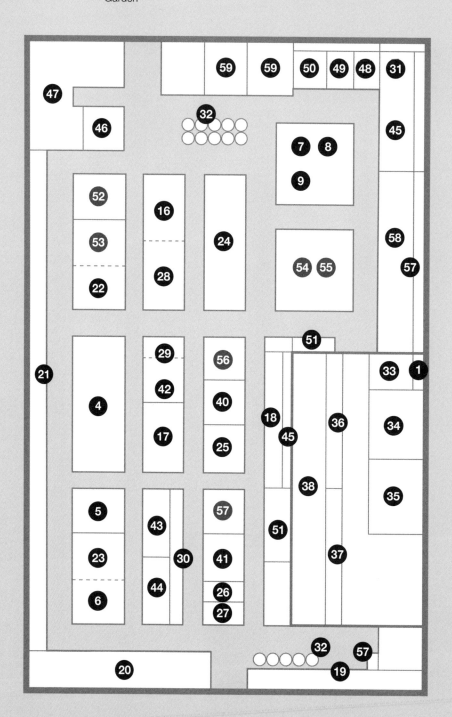

June

As soon as the month starts, you could be harvesting easily over a kilo of delicious fresh food every day in June. As well as greens, you'll be picking peas, beetroot, courgettes, carrots, spring onions, and lifting your first new potato crop. You can also plant out the rest of your tender crops now the risk of frost is truly over. But ensure you give these new transplants plenty of water within their first week or two, especially when the weather is warm and dry. If there is still plenty of pak choi in the hoop bed, clear the crop and process into a large kimchi to store in the fridge and enjoy eating over the next few months.

Key

Polytunnel
1. Coriander
33. Chillies
34. Aubergine
35. Cucumber
36. Basil
37. Tumbling tomatoes
38. Vine tomatoes

Hoop beds
52. New potatoes > **Chard**
53. Pak choi > **Dwarf beans**
22. Courgette
4. Potatoes
5. Beetroot
23. Dwarf beans
6. Cauliflower

Hot bed 1
7. Carrots
8. Spring onions
9. Turnips

Hot bed 2
54. Peas (for shoots), Lettuce, Spinach > **Cauliflower**
55. Radish, Pak choi > **Cucumbers**

Raised beds
46. Celery
16. Field beans
28. Napa cabbage
29. Leeks
42. Tree cabbage
17. New potatoes
30. Peas
43. Beetroot
44. Fennel
24. Onions
56. Turnip > **Kohlrabi**
40. Swede
25. Parsnips
57. Garlic > **Climbing beans**
41. Kohlrabi
26. Perpetual spinach
27. Radish
31. Shallots
45. Peas
58. Courgette

Salad bed
47. Salad leaves

Herb and edible flower bed
51. Edible flowers
18. Perennial herbs
45. Peas
50. Coriander
49. Parsley
48. Dill

Borders
57. Climbing beans
19. Jerusalem artichokes
20. Soft fruit
21. Spares bed
32. Potato pots

Compost bin
59. Winter squash

IN THE POLYTUNNEL

Beds
Tomatoes

These will now be growing rapidly. For vine tomatoes, **pinch out** the sideshoots that grow at 45 degrees from the main stem so the plant's energy is concentrated on growing upwards and creating abundant trusses of fruit. This also increases light and airflow. As the stems grow taller, continue to **wrap** them gently around the string that you attached to the top of the polytunnel frame last month (pictured below). Water vine and tumbling tomatoes regularly, and **feed** twice in June with homemade plant tea or seaweed feed (see p210). Instead of basil, **underplant** tomatoes with French marigolds to deter pests and attract beneficial insects, while adding some colour to the bed.

Basil

Plants will be producing abundant leaves this month so **harvest** regularly and keep well watered. Direct sow basil seed or transplant any extra seedlings underneath the tomatoes as a companion plant and to prolong the harvest.

Cucumbers, chillies, and aubergines

Keep well watered and **feed** as for tomatoes (cucumbers are pictured left).

Coriander

The few remaining plants will be flowering then setting seed. Harvest the delicious green seed and use in pickling or ferments.

ON THE SEEDLING SHELVES

Purple sprouting broccoli

Pot on to ensure seedlings continue developing before they are transplanted outside next month, once the peas have finished.

Crop	Sowing week	Cell type	Seeds per cell	Sowing depth	Cell count	Thin to
Climbing beans (after harvesting garlic)	1	Deep	1	3–4cm (1¼–1½in)	10	N/A
Kale	1	4cm (1½in)	2	0.5cm (¼in)	20	1
Winter cabbage	1	4cm (1½in)	2	2cm (¾in)	20	1
Fennel	2	4cm (1½in)	2	2cm (¾in)	20	1
Napa cabbage	2	4cm (1½in)	2	1cm (½in)	14	1
Purple sprouting broccoli (to polytunnel)	2	4cm (1½in)	2	2cm (¾in)	10	1
Spring onions	2	4cm (1½in)	5–6	1cm (½in)	20	N/A
Turnip	2	4cm (1½in)	3–4	2cm (¾in)	10	3
Winter squash (to hot bed)	2	7cm	2	0.5cm (¼in)	2	1
Coriander and dill	3	4cm (1½in)	4–6	2cm (¾in)	10 each	3–4
Dwarf beans	3	4cm (1½in)	1	2cm (¾in)	40	N/A

HOOP BEDS

Growth in these beds is truly abundant this month. Celebrate the end of the hungry gap as you harvest the first beetroot of the season and enjoy your first meal of freshly dug new potatoes. A single new potato plant will yield about 500–750g (1–1½lb) – enough for 2 generous servings. When you've harvested new potatoes, plant out the clumps of chard 15cm (6in) apart and water well. Ensure you **water** the potato hoop bed on a regular basis to maintain production and prevent disease (scab).

Towards the end of the month, you may also be able to **pick** your first cauliflower. It's also time to **clear** the remaining pak choi and **plant out** the dwarf beans sown in May, at 12–15cm (4¾–6in) apart.

HOT BEDS

Bed 1
Keep the bed well watered and continue to **pick** spring onions and carrots through June, but don't compost all the carrot tops. Use some to **make** a delicious pesto to enjoy with the new potatoes.

Bed 2
By the start of June, the hot bed may have produced around 6kg (13lb) of salad. Now, however, plants will be setting seed so **clear** any remaining plants and compost them. This frees up space to **transplant** 4 of the May sown cauliflowers spaced 50cm (20in) apart, as well as 6 outdoor cucumbers (pictured opposite, below right) on the north-facing edge. To maximize productivity, squeeze in a winter squash seedling to trail over the south-facing side of the bed.

RAISED BEDS

I love how full and green these beds are, with swede and parsnips growing strongly, peas in abundance, and the March new potatoes ready to **lift** when you've finished those in the hoop beds. A major **harvest** in June is garlic. After lifting the bulbs, plant out climbing beans in the space.

Peas
Pick sweet-tasting sugar snap peas regularly so plants continue to flower and develop new pods. If plants are sprawling, tie to the support with string.

Turnip
Harvest the largest turnips first to allow the smaller ones to mature.

Kohlrabi
Lift any tennis-ball-sized kohlrabi and enjoy roasted with a few herbs.

Tree cabbage
Harvest this quick-growing crop weekly, from mid-June. Water well to maintain production.

Perpetual spinach
You can keep picking this hugely productive green, but I recommend **allowing** the plant to grow on to get two harvests: large green leaves plus sweet crunchy stems. Harvest a few stems per plant and you'll get continuous cropping.

Field beans
Start harvesting the field beans (pictured below) as the pods swell and feel firm.

If any plants start to lean over, push in some sticks and tie string around them to keep them upright.

Courgettes
Transplant the May sown courgettes in front of the climbing beans, spaced 75cm (2½ft) apart, or you could replace 2 of the plants with the 2 winter squash (if you didn't plant one in the hot bed) for a winter crop.

Garlic
Garlic (pictured right) is traditionally pulled on the summer solstice. Hardneck garlic is ready to harvest when the bottom leaves start turning yellow, and softneck when the stems start to droop. Gently **uproot** the bulbs, brush off any soil, and tie in bunches of 6–7 stems. **Hang up** in the polytunnel to cure for 2 weeks, then store in a cool, dry place. Use the space to **construct** a wigwam and plant out the extra climbing beans at the end of June. Alternatively, sow 1 bean under each support 5cm (2in) deep.

SALAD BED

It's now time to **harvest** the first salads. Keep the bed very well watered to ensure good-quality plants and minimize the risk of bolting (flowering prematurely).

HERBS

Annuals
Keep picking dill, parsley, and coriander as needed. Then towards the end of June **sow** a new batch of coriander and dill either directly, or in modules. These will replace the current crops after they have flowered and set seed (pictured below). Parsley, which is a biennial, will continue to produce fresh leaves.

Perennials
Enjoy abundant harvests and **keep picking** leaves to use in the kitchen. With the exception of chives, which you can cut at the base for a second flush of leaves, the remaining perennial herbs will continue putting on huge amounts of growth this month.

EDIBLE FLOWERS

Borage, calendula, and nasturtium (pictured opposite) now enter full bloom and the petals add vibrant colour to summer salads. The flowers will attract many bees and other pollinators, bringing movement and sound to inject more life into the plot.

BORDERS

Climbing beans
Before you plant these out in early June in a long row, **construct** a support by making an A-frame for the raised bed against the south-facing border. Push in bamboo canes on both sides of the frame at 30cm (12in) intervals, and **transplant** one climbing bean seedling at the base of each. I also save some beans to plant out in the borders. Water well once transplanted.

Soft fruit
H**arvest** strawberries, currants and gooseberries when ripe, usually towards the end of the month (depending on your region).

Continue to **pick** rhubarb stems (pictured below, right) but leave at least 50 per cent of the plant untouched. I like to cook and freeze excess rhubarb for winter crumbles. Give the plants a generous **water**, with added liquid feed, near the end of June.

COMPOST

Use your bin as an extra bed and **transplant** the 2 winter squash seedlings in it. Make 2 30 x 30cm (12 x 12in) holes diagonally opposite each other and towards the corners of the bin. Fill these with compost, then plant the squashes, firm in, and **water** thoroughly. Encourage the plants to grow in opposite directions and you'll get a great yield come the autumn.

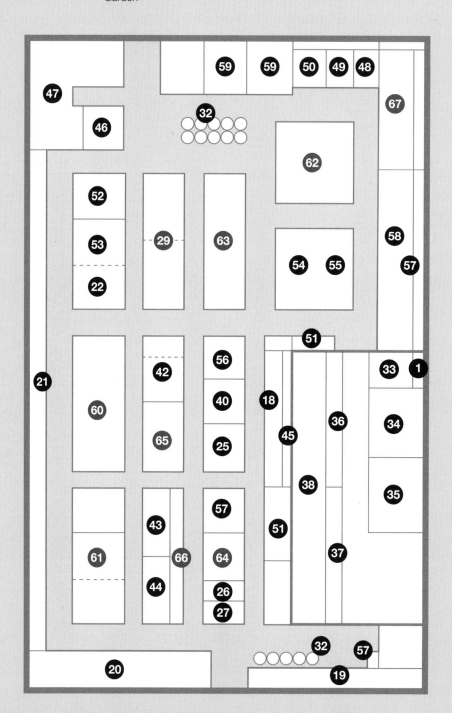

July

In July there is absolutely no need to buy vegetables or herbs. With the garden producing far more food than you can possibly eat fresh, it's the perfect time to start preserving to ensure an abundance of stored produce over the winter. For a range of options for the various crops, from roasting beetroot for the freezer and blanching cauliflower florets, to making kimchi, check out the In the Kitchen chapter and the Flavour Chart (see pp156–161). This month, potatoes and onions are important harvests, and it also marks the start of the tomato season. Harvesting these key staples, along with the garlic you lifted in June, represents a major milestone on the journey towards full self-sufficiency. July is also a very colourful month in the garden when the edible flowers in vibrant blues, yellows, and oranges, sing out among the different shades of green.

Key

Polytunnel
1. Coriander
33. Chillies
34. Aubergine
35. Cucumber
36. Basil
37. Tumbling tomatoes
38. Vine tomatoes

Hoop beds
52. Chard
53. Dwarf beans
22. Courgette
60. Potatoes > **Golden beetroot**
61. Beetroot, Dwarf beans, Cauliflower > **Carrots**

Hot bed 1
62. Carrots, Onions, Turnips > **Winter squash**

Hot bed 2
54. Cauliflower
55. Cucumbers

Raised beds
46. Celery
29. Field beans, Napa cabbage
> **Leeks**
42. Tree cabbage
65. New potatoes > **Kale**
66. Peas > **Napa cabbage**
43. Beetroot
44. Fennel
63. Onions > **Winter cabbage**
56. Kohlrabi
40. Swede
25. Parsnips
57. Climbing beans
64. Kohl rabi > **Fennel**
26. Perpetual spinach
27. Radish
67. Shallots, Peas > **Purple sprouting broccoli**
58. Courgette

Salad bed
47. Salad leaves

Herb and edible flower bed
51. Edible flowers
18. Perennial herbs
45. Peas
50. Coriander
49. Parsley
48. Dill

Borders
57. Climbing beans
19. Jerusalem artichokes
20. Soft fruit
21. Spares bed
32. Potato pots

Compost bin
59. Winter squash

IN THE POLYTUNNEL

Beds
Tomatoes

Continue to **prune** out sideshoots from the cordon tomatoes (pictured below). Remove any of the lower leaves below the first truss of fruit to maintain good airflow. Enjoy the first ripe tomatoes in a salad with some fresh leaves from the basil growing beneath, and remember to give plants a fortnightly homemade liquid or seaweed **feed** (see p210) to aid heavy cropping. Also, **mulch** around the base with grass clippings to maintain soil moisture. This will lessen the danger of the tomato skins splitting.

Cucumbers

Tie in cucumbers growing up a pyramid structure (pictured left). I do very little pruning this month but try to keep on top of harvesting cucumbers when ripe. If you are growing a variety that also produces male flowers (unlike a female-only hybrid), check your plants two to three times a week and remove these male blooms to avoid bitter cucumbers.

Chillies and aubergines

Water and feed regularly. Plants will start flowering and producing small fruits this month.

ON THE SEEDLING SHELVES

Purple sprouting broccoli

Pot on the purple sprouting intended for the polytunnel, that was sown in June, into 7cm (2¾in) pots at the end of this month. Sow pak choi.

Crop	Sowing week	Cell Type	Seeds per cell	Sowing depth	Cell count	Thin to
Pak choi	1	4cm (1½in)	2	1cm (½in)	40	1

HOOP BEDS

Potatoes and beetroot
Harvest the whole bed of potatoes on a dry day, spreading them (uncleaned) over a piece of fabric and leave them out, turning every couple of hours. In the early evening, transfer the sizeable harvest to hessian sacks (coffee shops using fresh beans are good sources), and store in a cool, dark, airy location. Next day, rake the bed thoroughly, water well, and apply a light layer (1–2cm/½–¾in) of compost, if you have any to hand. Make shallow rows 2cm (¾in) deep and 30cm (12in) apart along the bed and **direct sow** beetroot. The plants, protected by closing the hoop cover during cooler weather, will continue growing into autumn and the beets can be harvested throughout winter. Don't forget to keep these hoop beds watered.

Carrots
Harvest the dwarf beans, beetroot, and cauliflowers in the third hoop bed then **direct sow** the whole bed with carrots (pictured below). Follow the same bed preparation, row spacing, and depth as the direct-sown beetroot above. Utilize the plank method (see p31) for carrots to help with germination rates.

HOT BEDS

Bed 1
Continue to **harvest** spring onions and carrots. You can clear the entire bed of carrots this month, or just lift those in the top two corners closest to the climbing beans. In their place, **plant out** the two winter squash that were sown in June, one in each corner.

Bed 2
Make sure you keep the cauliflowers and quick-growing cucumber plants well watered. You can **support** the cucumbers by tying the trailing stems to canes or to netting pulled taut between two posts. Let the cucumber plants closest to the hot-bed sides sprawl over them and bear fruit.

RAISED BEDS

Onions and winter cabbage
Harvest onions towards the end of July, when the bulbs are a good size and the tops are still green (pictured right)

After lifting them, cut back the stems to leave just 3in (7cm) above the bulb. If the weather is dry, lay the onions out on the bed for a day, then gather up. Let the onions dry out throughly on the mini-greenhouse shelves or hang them upside down between wooden planks. Use the green tops to make a batch of pesto to freeze, or chop the stems into pieces then freeze on trays for 1–2 hours before storing in bags or containers. These will add flavour to soups and stews through autumn and winter.

With the onions cleared, use the space to **plant out** the winter cabbage sown in June, allowing 40cm (16in) between each plant.

Turnips and pak choi
Harvest any remaining turnips then, at the end of the month, **transplant** the pak choi, sown at the start of July, into the bed. Allow 25cm (10in) between the seedlings to give them room to grow large, plant in staggered rows spaced 20cm (8in) apart, and give them plenty of water over the next few weeks. Another option is to set aside some seedlings and **interplant** between the winter cabbage, harvesting the pak choi once the winter cabbages have started to crowd it out.

New potatoes and kale
Harvest the remaining new potatoes (pictured below) and replace with the

June-sown kale, spacing plants 35–40cm (14–16in) apart in diagonal rows and firming them in well with your hands (or feet). This will help the kale to remain upright during autumn and winter storms.

Field beans and leeks
Finish harvesting the field beans and compost the spent plants. It's now time to **transplant** the April sown leeks from the raised bed into the space. Using a fork, gently lift out the seedlings and place immediately in a bucket of water. This keeps them hydrated and makes separating the tangled roots much easier. Use a dibber to make holes 15–20cm (6–8in) deep, at a spacing

of 15cm (6in) apart. Then, **drop** a leek seedling into the base of each hole, water well, but don't push the soil back. With less resistance, the young leek stems will swell more easily. Where the leek seedlings were growing, **transplant** the 2 remaining tree cabbages. Then on the edge of the bed direct sow a row of spring onions spring thickly, 2cm (¾in) deep.

Peas and napa cabbage
Harvest the last of the peas, including those growing in the bed along with the beetroot and fennel. Replace these peas with a row of napa cabbage seedlings. **Plant** the seedlings **out** 35-40cm (12–16in) apart, plugging gaps with any remaining seedlings. **Clear** the spent peas that are growing behind the perennial herbs. In their place you can **transplant** any surplus kale seedlings 40cm (16in) apart along the back. Enjoy extra greens in winter and edible flower shoots in spring.

Shallots, peas, purple sprouting broccoli
Harvest the shallots and peas growing by the long row of climbing beans. In their place, **plant out** the first batch of purple sprouting broccoli, in two staggered rows 50cm (20in) apart.

Kohlrabi and fennel
Harvest the kohlrabi and use the space to **transplant** the Fennel sown last month in staggered rows. Allow 20cm (8in) between each plant and row.

Courgettes
Start to **harvest** the courgettes growing beneath the climbing beans this month. Pick the fruits little and often to enjoy them when young and tender.

SALAD BED

Continue harvesting as and when the salads are ready. If any are looking exhausted or have bolted, **clear** and **sow** fresh seed for a constant supply. Water the salad bed regularly to maintain leaf quality (every couple of days during dry weather).

HERBS

July is the month to sit back and enjoy abundant fresh herbs and their flowers (pictured left). **Pick** regularly, including those that are likely to have flowered and set seed, such as dill and coriander. Use fresh flowers and seed in the kitchen, and **set aside** seed to dry. For more fresh leaves, remove half of the original plants and **direct sow** additional dill and coriander in their place.

EDIBLE FLOWERS

To maintain production and prolong the vibrant colour, **deadhead** calendula flowers (pictured opposite) on a regular basis.

BORDERS

Soft fruit
The majority of the soft fruit will have finished cropping in July, and you can **preserve** any excess (see p182). But there will still be blackberries and autumn raspberries to look forward to. Not being nutrient-hungry plants, these berries won't need feeding.

Potato pots
Ensure these are well watered during dry weather.

COMPOST

Continue to **collect** materials to fill the second bin. In July, the first bin containing the two squashes planted last month will be completely covered by leaves and vines. **Apply** LAB and JMS amendments (see pp208–210) to this first bin to both speed up decomposition and improve nutrient supply to the hungry squash.

The
**Self-
Sufficiency**
Garden

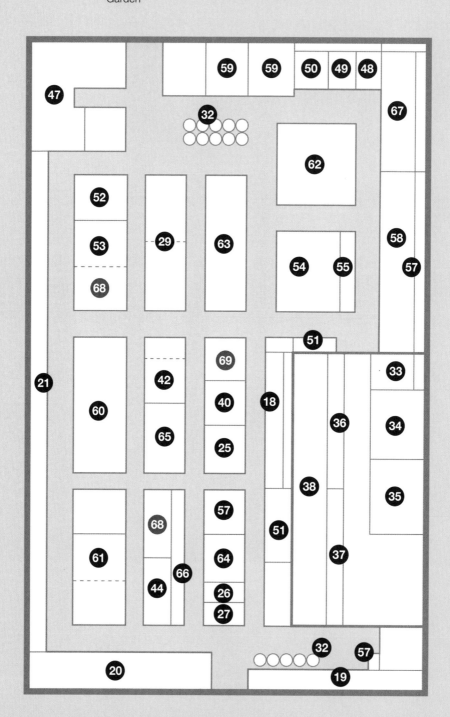

August

In August, a lovely month in the self-sufficiency garden, most of your time will be devoted to watering in the new plantings, harvesting delicious food, and keeping on top of the crops in the polytunnel. There will be masses of ripe tomatoes and cucumbers to pick every day, and plenty of produce to preserve for a welcome taste of summer in the darker months, including courgettes, climbing beans, and fennel. During August, I recommend you also check your cabbage plants, squishing any cabbage white caterpillars that would otherwise cause carnage, and give the whole garden at least one watering with diluted liquid feed. On late-summer days, the hot oranges and reds of the nasturtiums together with the sprawling squashes give an exotic, jungle-like feel to areas of the garden.

Key

Polytunnel
33. Chillies
34. Aubergine
35. Cucumber
36. Basil
37. Tumbling tomatoes
38. Vine tomatoes

Hoop beds
52. Chard
53. Dwarf beans
68. Courgette > **Daikon radish**
60. Golden beetroot
61. Carrots

Hot bed 1
62. Winter squash

Hot bed 2
54. Cauliflower
55. Cucumbers

Raised beds
29. Leeks
42. Tree cabbage
65. Kale
66. Napa cabbage
68. Beetroot > **Daikon radish**
44. Florence fennel
63. Winter cabbage
69. Kohl rabi > **Pak choi**
40. Swede
25. Parsnips
57. Climbing beans
64. Florence fennel
26. Perpetual spinach
27. Radish
58. Courgette
67. Purple sprouting broccoli

Salad bed
47. Salad leaves

Herb and edible flower bed
51. Edible flowers
18. Perennial herbs
50. Coriander
49. Parsley
48. Dill

Borders
57. Climbing beans
19. Jerusalem artichokes
20. Soft fruit
21. Spares bed
32. Potato pots

Compost bin
59. Winter squash

IN THE POLYTUNNEL

Beds
Tomatoes

Keep **picking** ripe tomatoes, preferably in the early morning so the fruits stay fresher for longer, and give them a liquid **feed** every two weeks. Cordon tomatoes (pictured below and opposite) will continue to send out sideshoots so prune these out regularly. When harvesting tomatoes, I also **remove** the leaves below the next fruit truss as I work my way up the stem from the bottom. This ensures strong airflow and lets in light to aid ripening.

Aubergines, chillies, cucumbers

Harvest aubergines, which are now at peak production, and feed as for tomatoes. **Pick** any ripe chillies but stop watering the plants from the fourth week of August: you'll be harvesting the majority of the crop next month. As you harvest your cucumbers, **remove** the older cucumber leaves this month to ward off potential disease and **prune** out any secondary vines, if there is no space for them on the

pyramid. Also snip off any large leaves blocking fruit from the sun and give the plants plenty of water.

Basil

It's vital to keep the soil around basil roots from drying out, so **water** well and remove flowers so the plants producie more leaves.

ON THE SEEDLING SHELVES

Purple sprouting broccoli

Before these replace the cucumbers in the polytunnel, **pot on** the June seedlings for a second time into 10–12cm (4–4¾in) pots. Use soil from the garden to fill the pots and move this crop into the cold frame. The plants will prefer the outside temperatures – and leave the lid open.

Crop	Sowing week	Cell type	Seeds per cell	Sowing depth	Cell count	Thin to
Winter radish	2	4cm (1½in)	4–5	2cm (¾in)	40	N/A
Spring cabbage	2	4cm (1½in)	2	2cm (¾in)	20	1
Chard	3	4cm (1½in)	3–4	2cm (¾in)	20	3
Napa cabbage	3	4cm (1½in)	2	2cm (¾in)	20	1

HOOP BEDS

Keep **watering** and keep the hoop beds propped open by day (pictured opposite) and night. **Harvest** dwarf beans and **pull up** the 2 courgette plants around mid-month. Use the space to **direct sow** 4 rows of daikon radish 2cm (¾in) deep, spacing one seed every 2cm (¾in) and allowing 15cm (6 in) between rows. **Water** thoroughly and when the seedlings appear, thin to 1 plant every 5–6cm (2–2½in) to give the roots enough space to grow huge.

HOT BEDS

The only task this month is to keep harvesting.

RAISED BEDS

Harvest crops, such as fennel, as and when you need them, focusing on the larger specimens first to allow the smaller ones to develop. You'll also notice this month that winter crops, such as swede and leeks, are maturing quickly, as is the squash. Although the large plants in these beds are helping to smother weeds, it's still worth doing a weekly **weed** to keep on top of any that do emerge.

Beetroot and daikon
Harvest the remaining beetroot, and direct sow five to six rows of daikon radish in their place with the same depth and spacing as for hoop beds (see left). You'll get excellent winter harvests to preserve into kimchi.

Celery
Harvest the remaining celery transplanted in late May and plant out spare seedlings in the space.

SALAD BED

August is an excellent month to refresh the salad bed. **Remove** tired crops and add a 1–2cm (½ –¾in) layer of compost. **Direct sow** winter lettuce, rocket, oriental greens, and napa cabbage for harvests into autumn before the winter salads in the polytunnel are ready.

HERBS

Keep picking perennial herbs (pictured below and right) and **direct sow** more dill and coriander. It's your last opportunity to do so before autumn.

EDIBLE FLOWERS

Keep deadheading flowers but allow the nasturtiums to set seed. Collect the seeds and preserve them in vinegar. They make a good substitute for capers.

BORDERS

Climbing beans
Pick regularly and water.

Soft fruit
Net cultivated blackberries before they ripen to keep the birds off. If you haven't grown any, forage for wild hedgerow berries to freeze for winter use.

COMPOST

Nothing to be done here in August.

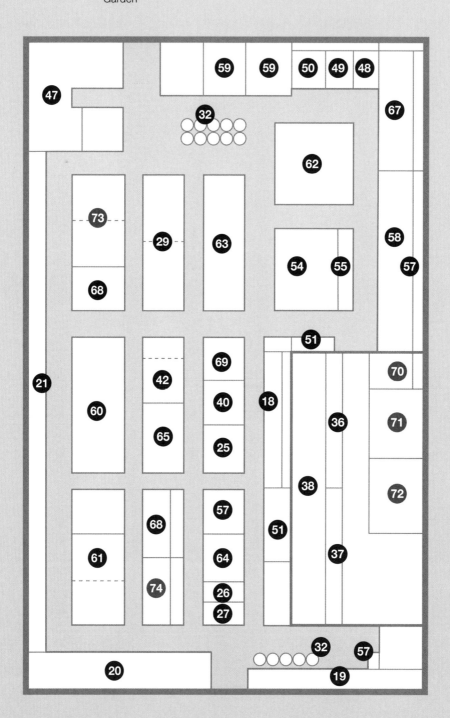

September

September brings cooler weather and a feeling of calm before autumn sets in, but the garden is still abundant. The chillies are ready to harvest, tomatoes continue to ripen, the first winter squashes make an appearance, and you'll be planting out some of the last of this year's crops. A key focus this month should be soil and plant health, and I would highly recommend applying JMS (see p210) wherever possible, as well as giving all the beds at least one liquid feed. You can save time by applying both in the same application: start with the JMS then top up with feed instead of diluting with water. Some of the older leaves on plants such as brassicas and climbing beans may be turning yellow, so trim these off to maintain healthy, vibrant-looking crops.

Key

Polytunnel
70. Chillies > **Chard**
71. Aubergine > **Napa cabbage**
72. Cucumber > **Purple sprouting broccoli**
36. Basil
37. Tumbling tomatoes
38. Vine tomatoes

Hoop beds
73. Chard, Dwarf beans
> **Spring cabbage**
68. Daikon radish
60. Golden beetroot
61. Carrots

Hot bed 1
62. Winter squash

Hot bed 2
54. Cauliflower
55. Cucumbers

Raised beds
29. Leeks
42. Tree cabbage
65. Kale
68. Daikon radish
74. Napa cabbage, Florence fennel
> **Winter radish**
63. Winter cabbage
69. Pak choi
40. Swede
25. Parsnips
57. Climbing beans
64. Florence fennel
26. Perpetual spinach
27. Radish
58. Courgette
67. Purple sprouting broccoli

Salad bed
47. Salad leaves

Herb and edible flower bed
51. Edible flowers
18. Perennial herbs
50. Coriander
49. Parsley
48. Dill

Borders
57. Climbing beans
19. Jerusalem artichokes
20. Soft fruit
21. Spares bed
32. Potato pots

Compost bin
59. Winter squash

IN THE POLYTUNNEL

Beds

The polytunnel is one of the busiest areas of the garden in September. **Harvest** ripe chillies (pictured opposite) to dry or freeze, and **pick** the last aubergines (below) and cucumbers, setting some aside to preserve and eat in the months ahead.

Use the space to **transplant** the chard and napa cabbage from the seedling shelves, and the purple sprouting broccoli from the cold frame. Allow 15cm (6in) between each chard seedling to give you smallish leaves over winter, 35–40cm (14–16in) for the napa cabbage, and 40–45cm (16–18in) for the purple sprouting broccoli.

If you have any spare napa cabbage or chard seedlings, **plant** these out underneath the tomatoes.

Tomatoes

Continue to **harvest** and **prune** sideshoots from tomatoes as they ripen. The bush types may stop producing this month, so **pull up** the plants and put

them on the compost heap. Cooling temperatures mean less watering in the polytunnel, giving you more time to focus on nurturing those delicious tomatoes.

ON THE SEEDLING SHELVES

September is the perfect time to **sow** winter salads. These will be planted out in the polytunnel next month to replace the tomatoes. The sowing list below comprises my usual selection of salads. They will give you fresh leaves over winter through until March or April, when the plants start to run to seed. But by spring, the hot-bed salads will start to come into production, and the combination will provide you with full year-round salad self-sufficiency. A variety of salad crops is vital because their leaves grow incredibly slowly (and sometimes not at all during December and January). Growing this selection and quantity of salad leaves will allow you to **harvest** from each type without overpicking.

Crop	Sowing week	Cell type	Seeds per cell	Sowing depth	Cell count	Thin to
Claytonia	2	4cm (1½in)	3–4	1cm (½in)	20	N/A
Coriander (for winter salads)	2	4cm(1½in)	5–6	2cm (¾in)	20	4
Mizuna	2	4cm (1½in)	2	1cm (½in)	20	1
Purslane	2	4cm (1½in)	3–4	1cm (½in)	20	N/A
Radish	2	4cm (1½in)	3–4	2cm (¾in)	20	N/A
Rocket	2	4cm (1½in)	3–4	1cm (½in)	20	N/A
Winter lettuce	2	4cm (1½in)	3	1cm (½in)	20	1
Peas for shoots	3	4cm (1½in)	3	2cm (¾in)	40	N/A

HOOP BEDS

Harvest any remaining dwarf beans, then clear and compost them (pictured below). In their place **plant out** the spring cabbage seedlings sown last month, allowing 30cm (12in) between plants in staggered rows 30cm (12in) apart. These will supplement the tree cabbage in the raised beds providing fresh green leaves during the upcoming "hungry gap" (see p148). Close the hoop beds on cool nights (below 8°C/46°F).

HOT BEDS

Bed 1
Snip off any leaves blocking the ripening squashes and keep them well watered.

Bed 2
Pull up the cucumber plants as they stop producing, and **harvest** any cauliflowers of a suitable size. The gaps won't now be filled. Instead, the compost is left and allowed to break down until November, when

you clear the bed and use the contents as a mulch.

RAISED BEDS

Keep harvesting pak choi, perpetual spinach, and climbing beans, then **clear** the remaining fennel (pictured right). A fantastic crop for preserving, fennel is delicious either fermented or pickled to enjoy over late autumn and winter.

Transplant the August sown winter radish seedlings in its place, allowing 25cm (10in) between each clump in staggered rows 20cm (8in) apart. The generous spacing ensures maximum light so you get good-sized roots in late autumn to early winter.

SALAD BED

Harvest leaves as you need them and compost any plants that are no longer productive. **Don't sow** any further salad crops outside as it's almost the end of their growing season.

HERBS

Coriander and dill
Leave the flowering plants (dill is pictured left) in situ this month and delay removing them until early winter. This allows the herbs to set seed and drop it onto the ground below, resulting in a small forest of dill and coriander seedlings next season with no effort on your part. All you'll need to do is thin them and **transplant** elsewhere.

Borage, calendula, nasturtium
Don't **deadhead** and **allow** the seeds to drop. When seedlings appear next

of rodent damage (which I spotted in one of my pots). **Tip out** the plants into a wheelbarrow (pictured opposite), collect the tubers, and **dry** in the polytunnel for a day (turning them over a few times) before storing in a hessian bag in a cool, dry, dark place.

COMPOST

Activity around the bins will increase next month but all you need to do this month is **keep adding** spent crops and garden waste to the third bin (the bin without the squash plants growing in it), supplementing it with material you have sourced from elsewhere.

spring, they can planted out or potted up and taken to plant swaps to save costs.

BORDERS

Strawberries
The rest of the soft fruit doesn't need any attention this month, but early in September is a great time to **pot up** plantlets growing at the tip of strawberry runners. Keep these attached to the mother plant for at least 4 weeks

then **sever** the runner and grow them on. Plantlets are also ideal for taking to plant swaps.

Raspberries
Harvest the autumn raspberries when ripe (pictured above), and add any poor-quality fruits to the compost heap.

Potato pots
You can begin to **harvest** this crop in September, especially if you spot signs

The
Self-
Sufficiency
Garden

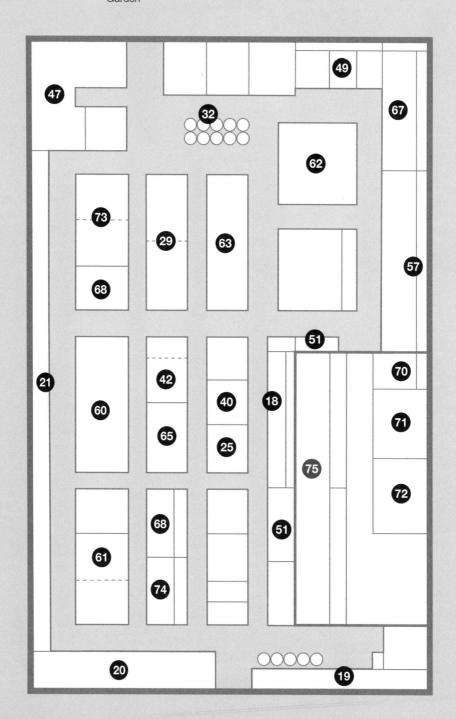

October

After mellow September, the month of October brings much colder nights and, for many, the increased risk of frost signifies the end of the growing season. Be vigilant, take note of the weather forecast, and always close the polytunnel doors and hoop beds at night to protect any tender crops. Tomatoes and climbing beans should keep cropping until the end of the month, and there will be winter squash and leafy greens to harvest. With less to do on the plot and self-sufficiency uppermost in your mind, October is the ideal time to batch cook, make preserves, and freeze produce. You'll be rewarded with plenty of stored food to supplement the winter crops still growing. Finally, October is a great month to focus on composting, which I cover at the end of this section.

Key

Polytunnel
70. Chard
71. Napa cabbage
72. Purple sprouting
75. Basil, Tumbling tomatoes, Vine tomatoes> **Winter salads**

Hoop beds
73. Spring cabbage
68. Daikon radish
60. Golden beetroot
61. Carrots

Hot bed 1
62. Winter squash

Raised beds
29. Leeks
42. Tree cabbage
65. Kale
68. Daikon radish
74. Winter radish
63. Winter cabbage
40. Swede
25. Parsnips
67. Purple sprouting broccoli

Salad bed
47. Salad leaves

Herb and edible flower bed
51. Edible flowers
18. Perennial herbs
49. Parsley

Borders
19. Jerusalem artichokes
20. Soft fruit
21. Spares bed
32. Potato pots
57. Climbing beans

IN THE POLYTUNNEL

Beds
Tomatoes and salads
Continue to **harvest** tomatoes until the end of the month, including any green fruits (pictured opposite). Either ripen these indoors or make a batch of green tomato chutney. In mid-October, **plant out** the salad crops you sowed last month (pictured above). I like to put some under the tomato plants, adding a small handful of compost to each transplant hole. At the end of the month, I cut down the tomato plants but leave the roots in the ground to break down and improve fertility for the salads. Space the remaining salad plants randomly, leaving 20–25cm (8–10in) between each.

ON THE SEEDLING SHELVES

With the salads cleared, the shelves will be empty for the first time since March. One option is to **dismantle** and store them temporarily so you can use the indoor space as a sheltered work or sitting area over winter.

HOOP BEDS

Water the spring cabbages, radish, carrots and beetroot, and remember to keep the covers on at night now temperatures have dropped.

HOT BEDS

Lift the last squashes this month (pictured p124). There is nothing more to harvest from these two hot beds, but they will have provided me with over 45kg (101lbs) of food. **Clear** any remaining plants from the hot beds and leave them empty. The organic material will continue breaking down ready to be spread as mulch (see p125).

RAISED BEDS

Winter radish will have grown after September's warmth, as will swede and leeks (pictured opposite). I usually give the beds their last diluted liquid **feed** in the first half of the month. This supplements the slowing growth before winter sets in.

Climbing beans

Most of the fresh beans will have been harvested by the end of September, but you can leave the remaining pods on the plant to dry naturally Stored in airtight containers, they make an excellent bulk ingredient for soups, stews, and casseroles over winter. If autumn is wet, it's best to harvest the beans and pod them (pictured below). Then spread out the beans on a mesh rack to air dry on a sunny windowsill indoors

for two weeks before storing. Reserve some dried beans to sow next year.

SALAD BED

After harvesting the last leaves of the season, **cut down** any remaining top growth at the end of the month and **compost**. Leave the roots in the ground to break down. This will add some goodness to the soil but you can further increase fertility by sowing a cover crop, which will protect the soil over winter. I would recommend you **direct sow** field beans (pictured below, right) or vetch to fix nitrogen in the soil ready for more productive salad growing next year.

HERBS AND FLOWERS

Clear all the annual flowering plants at the end of October but **collect and save** any seed (pictured below, left). Spread the seed out on a baking sheet and leave indoors on a sunny windowsill for two weeks, before storing it in labelled paper envelopes. **Compost** the remaining plant material.

Perennials
Mint, lemon balm, and oregano are now starting to die back before going into winter dormancy. Allow the stems to dry out before you **cut them** down to 2–3 cm (¾–1¼in) above soil level to keep the herb bed tidy. **Leave** the remaining perennial herbs to stand over winter.

BORDERS

Jerusalem artichokes
After flowering (pictured opposite), these plants will begin to die back but **leave**

the stems standing. Don't cut them down, so they can dry out completely. The tubers won't be ready to dig up and use until November onwards

Strawberries
At the end of the month, **sever** the strawberry runners (pictured opposite) you potted up in September from their mother plants. **Plant out** straight away, or **move** the pots into the cold frame over winter to swap or give away next spring. Don't forget to **water** them.

Potato pots
If you haven't yet harvested your potatoes, and if there is the threat of frost, **transfer** the potato plants into the polytunnel to allow the tubers to continue developing. The plants will continue to naturally die back so keep them in their pots and **harvest** tubers as and when needed.

COMPOST

One of the best ways to bulk out your compost is to **spread** fallen autumn leaves over the lawn then run the mower over them. The resulting mix of grass and leaves makes a perfect blend of greens and browns that you can immediately **add** to the third bin, which should be full by the end of October. If you grew winter squash in one of the other two bins, **harvest** them this month and **top up** the bin with additional material. Aim to have this completely full by December, and **mix** the fresher top layers with existing material once the bin is full.

As for the first compost bin, **inspect** the contents and if the original material is still recognizable, **turn** it thoroughly to speed up decomposition. If, however, the material is well decomposed, **cover** the heap with cardboard until you are ready to use it.

The hot beds (pictured below) are also integral to the composting strategy for the self-sufficiency garden. They will provide most of material needed to mulch your raised beds either later in autumn or over the winter months. To supercharge their contents and those of the other bins with beneficial bacteria, **remove** any cardboard covering and thoroughly **drench** the piles with diluted LAB (see p208). Then **cover** with cardboard to prevent saturation by rain. Excessive moisture will slow down the composting process.

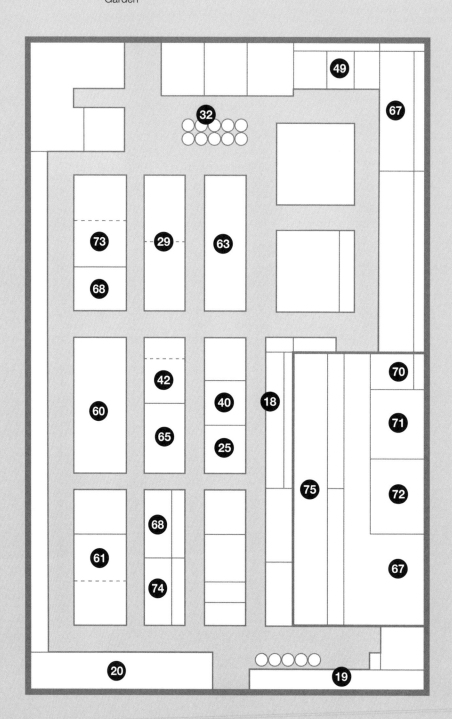

Into Winter

I often joke that November is like a summer holiday for gardeners; it's a time to take things easy. Any remaining plants will either have been cleared, or left for harvesting over winter and early spring next year. In theory, you could leave the garden for a whole month – even the polytunnel, if the doors are wedged open just a crack.

From now until late February is a quiet period when you'll be enjoying your winter crops, including leeks, Jerusalem artichokes, brassicas, swedes, parsnips, and appreciating their different flavours. I also use this time to make a start on preparations for the next growing season, paying particular attention to soil fertility by mulching all the beds with homemade compost. I also find that dedicating one evening a week to reading gardening books and watching videos is a great way to gain inspiration and ideas for next year's growing journey.

Key

Polytunnel
70. Chard
71. Napa cabbage
72. Purple sprouting broccoli
75. Winter salads

Hoop beds
73. Spring cabbage
60. Golden beetroot
61. Carrots
68. Daikon radish

Raised beds
29. Leeks
42. Tree cabbage
65. Kale
68. Daikon radish
74. Winter radish
63. Winter cabbage
40. Swede
25. Parsnips
67. Purple sprouting broccoli

Herb and edible flower bed
18. Perennial herbs
49. Parsley

Borders
19. Jerusalem artichokes
20. Soft fruit
32. Potato pots

IN THE POLYTUNNEL

With the onset of shorter days and cooler temperatures, crops under cover need far less water. Under-watering, rather than over-watering, is one way to avoid excessive moisture build-up, which can lead to mould and plants rotting. Also, don't forget to **ventilate** the polytunnel over winter. Unless there is a prolonged cold spell or a hard frost is forecast, I keep both doors half-open.

I usually **water** all the plants in the tunnel deeply, once or twice in November, but only once per month from December to February unless the top 5cm (2in) of soil feels bone dry. I also recommend you regularly **check** all the plants and promptly address any pest or disease issues (see p146) that may arise.

Harvest winter salads as and when needed, taking only a few leaves from each plant so they continue to produce (pictured below). **Pick** fresh napa cabbage from late autumn onwards, and enjoy delicious purple sprouting broccoli from the end of winter into early spring. If you moved the container potatoes into the polytunnel, these can be harvested as needed.

From mid-February, start to **sow** crops in modules ready to transplant in the hoop beds in four to six weeks. Onion sets, peas, radish, turnip, field beans, beetroot, as well as cauliflower and cabbage, will provide important harvests during the "hungry gap", and all respond well to a head start. To aid germination, **add** a layer of bubble wrap around the mini-greenhouse in the polytunnel if it doesn't have its own cover.

HOOP BEDS

Watering requirements drop from November onwards, so **follow** the watering strategy for the polytunnel. Although crops in these beds are hardy, you can prolong their productivity by covering them each evening, but **ventilate** during the day by propping the covers open with a block of wood. **Harvest** daikon radish (pictured opposite), carrots (pictured below), and beetroot as needed, and allow the spring cabbage to continue developing.

HOT BEDS

Use a fork to lift and **check** how the material in the hot beds is breaking down. **Bag up** any ready compost in sacks to use when needed, or to spread as a mulch (see **Adding fertility**, p131). If the material in both beds hasn't broken down sufficiently, **empty** one bed and pile the contents on top of the material in the other bed. The extra mass will help decomposition and you'll get finished compost for mulching before the end of winter.

Gather material for next year's crops in December and January and check out potential sources of bulk organic matter, such as a local stables for horse manure. **Collect** and store autumn leaves in bags, remembering to make holes

in the bottom first, or use coffee sacks. The leaves are an excellent source of carbon to mix with nitrogen-rich manure that has very little straw, or with seaweed. See pages 136–137 for mid-February sowing suggestions.

RAISED BEDS

Garlic
The best time to **plant** garlic cloves for a reliable harvest is late autumn to early winter. (pictured above, right). Dedicate at least one third of a raised bed to next year's crop and plant the cloves 5cm (2in) deep, with 10cm (4in) between each, in staggered rows 7.5cm (3in) apart.

Harvest pak choi, the remaining napa cabbage (pictured opposite, top), and some of the winter radish in early November, and continue harvesting kale and tree cabbage. The first swede (pictured opposite, bottom) may be ready to lift at the end of the month.

During winter, **lift** leeks as you need them and **harvest** kale, tree cabbage, and parsnips (pictured above, left).

BORDERS

Jerusalem artichokes are now ready to harvest, as well as any container potatoes that are growing outside.

ADDING FERTILITY WITH COMPOST

The quiet period from November through to late winter presents the perfect opportunity to **mulch** all your growing spaces with a layer of homemade compost in preparation for the next growing season. Compost adds valuable organic matter that is full of nutrients as well as carbon, both of which are essential for soil health and fertility. Organic matter also improves the soil's capacity to hold water so plants are kept hydrated for longer.

Homemade compost
Your compost should be fully decomposed, have a crumbly texture, and smell earthy – like a forest floor. **Remove** large pieces of woody or fibrous material, such as brassica stems, before you **spread** the compost as a mulch. There's no need to sieve it – that's only necessary when you're sowing seeds.

Mulching raised vegetable beds

Aim to **spread** a layer of mulch at least 2.5cm (1in) deep over all the beds, including the hoop and polytunnel beds. To cover each square metre (10 square feet) of growing space to that depth, you'll need 25 litres (5½ gallons) of compost; for a 3cm (1¼in) covering you will need 30 litres (6½ gallons). When mulching I use a 30-litre (6½-gallon) bucket to carry the compost to the beds (pictured opposite).

Spreading a layer of compost over beds that have been cleared is straightforward, but some will still have crops, such as tree cabbage and kale, growing in them. First, I recommend you **calculate** how much compost you need to mulch the bed, then **distribute** it evenly over the the surface and around the plants. For winter crops that are growing close together, such as leeks, this isn't practical so wait until you've harvested, then immediately mulch with compost.

If you have excess compost, add a layer up to 5cm (2½in) deep. If you lack compost, even a 1cm (½in) mulch will help. A useful formula to know, is that each 1cm (½in) increase of depth per square

metre will require 10 litres (2¼ gallons) of compost. This is especially useful when calculating how much compost you'll need to buy in, although hopefully this amount will be minimal. A standard size raised bed, 3m x 1.2m (10ft x 4ft) will need about four 30-litre (6½-gallon) buckets of compost annually.

Mulching perennial beds

Compost is a precious resource and best used on annual vegetable beds. Perennial vegetables, herbs, and soft fruit can be mulched with seaweed, leaves, woodchip, and well-rotted animal manure. All four materials will continue to decompose after application, so **spread** a thicker layer of at least 5cm (2in) deep on the surface as a mulch. **Work around** the plants and keep the stems 2cm (¾in) clear of any mulch to ensure good airflow and prevent moisture build-up.

Chicken manure

If you don't have sufficient homemade compost to mulch your beds, I suggest you **add** pelleted chicken manure. It's a natural, low-cost way to enrich the soil and a great short-term solution. You'll need 100g (3½oz) of pellets per square metre of ground and they can be applied over autumn

and winter. **Sprinkle** them over the soil and lightly **rake** in but, as with the mulches for perennial beds, **keep them away** from the stems of any crops still growing in the soil. In coming growing seasons, you can **top up** nutrient supplies when the beds are at their most productive, by adding a further 50g (1¾oz) of pellets per square metre of ground in late June/early July.

FORWARD PLANNING

Through the autumn and winter months, I like to review the past growing season and then come up with ways to make the next one even more productive. Take time to fine-tune your next season's planting plan, research new varieties before putting in your seed order, and get inspiration from books and videos. Learning from the successes and challenges of the previous growing season is easily the best way to make progress on your journey towards self-sufficiency.

The Second Season

Now that you have the first growing season under your belt, take time to evaluate your approach to the second season. Repeat growing techniques that produced good yields last season, but make any necessary amendments to anything that didn't go according to plan. Aim to treat next season as an opportunity to try new varieties and learn new techniques, so you get the maximum from your plot. For me, this new growing season starts in February with early sowings in the polytunnel and hot beds. These sowings will provide plenty of food during the so-called hungry gap (see p148) when there is little in the outside beds.

PLANTING

Creating a monthly planting plan is the most effective method for ensuring consistent harvests through the year, and I've shared my plan for the first year of the self-sufficiency garden. At the start of each month, there is a simple diagram of the layout of the garden spaces. Each space is also annotated to indicate which crop is growing there, and whether the crop will be harvested and replaced with another. A clear, uncomplicated plan can help you keep track, save time, and ensure maximum productivity in the garden. I've deliberately kept mine simple to make it easy to follow and for quick reference month by month.

As with every new season's planting plan, my goal is to ensure every bit of space of the garden is planted by May, and remains full until November. And I always create my planting plan on paper, using a pencil, because there will be a lot of adjustments to make as the plan gets filled in. Also, don't forget that some crops from last year will occupy space into the second growing season and need to be clearly marked on the plan. To help you plan ahead, the chart opposite identifies these crops. It shows when you can expect to harvest the last of them and then you can clear the space ready for the next planting.

Crop	Last harvest
Purple sprouting broccoli (under cover)	Early April
Purple sprouting (outside bed)	Early May
Leeks	Late April
Kale	Mid-May (after picking flower shoots)
Tree cabbage	Late May or keep in place*
Spring cabbage	Mid–late May
Garlic	Late June
Winter salads (under cover)	Mid-April
Chard (under cover)	Mid-April

*If you remove all the flower shoots from tree cabbage, it will continue to grow for another season.

YIELDS

When creating a planting plan, consider how much food you are aiming to produce in the space you have available.

To help you with quantities, I've included a guide that offers average yields and plant numbers per square metre (see pp142–144). It is based on my own harvests so expect some variation from your yields. However, I hope it proves to be a very useful starting point for your own planting plan and helps you understand how much your crops can produce.

IN THE POLYTUNNEL

Find a few hours in early February to organize everything in preparation for spring. Check your tools, arrange stored pots and module trays neatly, ensure your watering system is working well, and finally wash the inside and outside of the polytunnel with warm soapy water to remove any algae and let in maximum light. Clean the hoop bed covers in the same way.

HOT BEDS

Bed 1
Aim to fill your first hot bed with material collected over winter and sow it by mid-February. In the first season, the beds were sown in March but with the beds up

and running you can sow two weeks earlier and harvest your first salads by mid- to late March. Either follow last year's hot-bed sowing guide (see p52 March) or choose from the following crops, which can all be sown in February: lettuce, rocket, radish, spinach, pea shoots, pak choi, spring onions, beetroot, dill, coriander, carrots, chard, and turnips.

Don't forget to use the space between the rows of seedlings, when they emerge, to germinate tender crops such as aubergines, chillies, and tomatoes, as well as starting off seed modules of crops to be planted out in beds in March and April.

COMPOST

Making compost in the second season follows a similar pattern to the first season. Fill one of the compost bins by mid-May at the latest, so you can plant one or two squash seedlings there in June to maximize space. Fill up the other two bins as material becomes available from your garden, household, friends, and local community.

VARIETY TRIALS

Every garden reflects the taste of its gardener. Taking time to trial different crop varieties to suit your needs allows you to personalize your growing area. Yet this needn't mean finding additional space. Simply sow half a row of a different parsnip variety, or plant just 10 sets of a different variety of onion. If the trial variety doesn't perform well then any loss is minimal, but you get an added bonus if it outperforms your regular variety. Over time you'll develop your own bespoke collection of go-to staple crop varieties. I would also encourage those with larger plots to dedicate an area of 1–2 sq m (10–20 sq ft) per year to trial new crops for possible inclusion in future planting plans.

UPSKILLING

To my mind, acquiring a range of complementary skills is the best way to make progress on your self-sufficiency journey. With an ability to cook as well as grow food, you can create delicious meals with your fresh produce. A knowledge of preserving techniques will also allow you to store it. But if you aren't familiar with preserving, consider learning

about lacto-fermentation before the new season gets underway. That way, you can process your harvests and enjoy nutritious food over winter. You could also sign up for a day's foraging course to see what grows wild in your local area and use it to supplement your homegrown produce.

MULTI-FUNCTIONAL SPACE

According to one of my favourite gardening sayings, the best fertilizer is the gardener's shadow. The more time you spend in the garden, the more tender loving care your plants will receive. Take your cuppa into the garden and you might note slug damage on the salads that needs dealing with, or see a climbing bean that's come loose from its support. A garden, no matter how productive, should also be a place where you can escape, relax, and just enjoy being outside.

Before each new growing season, I like to find one additional element I can add to the garden to increase my enjoyment of the space and make it multi-functional. A kitchen garden lends itself beautifully to a range of related activities and I've listed a few ideas below, including some that can be adapted for small spaces.

> Firepit (pictured opposite)
> Pizza oven (portable)
> Reading corner
> Storm kettle (pictured below)
> Breakfast/evening drinks table (foldaway)
> Oak-barrel ice bath

> Dartboard
> Bird table
> Outdoor easel
> Cut flower bed

KEEP TRACK

Documenting as much of what happens in the garden as possible is a great habit to get into and will help you feel even more connected to your growing space. I find that a diary, camera, tape measure, and weighing scales (to note down yields) serve as excellent kit for making a record of the growing year. You can then review everything over winter and the notes and photos will be invaluable when trying to set objectives or capture your dreams for the following season.

CROP GROWING SPACE AND YIELD

This crop yield factsheet is designed to help you maximize your planting plans by showing how many plants you can grow per square metre and the average yield you can expect crop by crop. I opted for a square-metre approach as this is a measurement that most of the self-sufficiency garden can be split into. The factsheet uses my own harvest data over the last few years, and should be seen as a guide to approximately how much your garden could yield over the year. The crops listed are annuals only, and also include crops not grown in the first season of the self-sufficiency garden. I've included them to give you enough information to grow these other crops, too.

Note on planting space

The spacing measurements are an average appropriate for block planting and may differ slightly from specifics in the book, but it really doesn't matter too much!

If a crop is better suited to planting in rows, refer to the spacing between plants. Block planting strikes a balance between space per plant and yield. It allows more space, which avoids overcrowding plants or reducing light levels. Aim to plant in staggered rows, giving the same spacings to all plants.

Crop	Spacing between plants and between rows (cm)	Yield per plant (g)*	Plants per square metre	Square metre yield average (g)
Aubergine	50	1500	4	**6,000**
Basil	10	100	20	**2,000**
Bean, broad	20	175	20	**3,500**
Bean, dwarf	15	90	30	**2,700**
Bean, field	20	200	20	**4,000**
Bean, climbing	30	550	10	**5,500**
Bean, French climbing	30	375	10	**3,750**
Beetroot	20	175	30	**5,250**
Broccoli, calabrese	50	450	4	**1,800**
Broccoli, purple sprouting	50	400	4	**1,600**
Brussels sprouts	40	1,000	6	**6,000**
Cabbage, spring	35	800	7	**5,600**

Crop	Spacing between plants and between rows (cm)	Yield per plant (g)*	Plants per square metre	Square metre yield average (g)
Cabbage, summer	40	1,200	5	6,000
Cabbage, winter	40	1,200	5	6,000
Cabbage, napa	35	800	8	6,400
Cabbage, tree	40	1,000	6	6,000
Carrots	7.5	100	100	10,000
Cauliflower	50	1,500	4	6,000
Celeriac	30	750	10	7,500
Celery	30	600	10	6,000
Chard	15	350	20	7,000
Chicory	20	225	20	4,500
Chillies	40	300	5	1,500
Coriander	10	35	20	700
Courgettes	75	4,000	1	4,000
Cucumbers	30	4,000	6	24,000
Fennel	20	225	20	4,500
Garlic	10	90	40	3,600
Jerusalem artichokes	30	1,200	8	9,600
Kale	30	750	8	6,000
Kohlrabi	15	225	25	5,625
Leeks	15	200	40	8,000
Oca (New Zealand yam)	30	400	8	3,200
Onions	15	250	35	8,750
Pak choi	25	350	15	5,250
Parsley	15	50	10	500
Parsnips	10	250	40	10,000

Crop	Spacing between plants and between rows (cm)	Yield per plant (g)*	Plants per square metre	Square metre yield average (g)
Peas	10	150	50	7,500
Peppers	40	300	5	1,500
Potatoes, new	30	800	7	5,600
Potatoes, second earlies	30	1,200	6	7,200
Potatoes, maincrop	40	1,800	5	9,000
Pumpkin	90	5,000	1	5,000
Radish	10	20	100	2,000
Radish, daikon	10	250	40	10,000
Rocket	10	25	40	1,000
Salsify	10	150	40	6,000
Salad leaves (including lettuce)	10	150	50	7,500
Shallots	10	150	40	6,000
Spinach	10	150	40	6,000
Spinach, perpetual	20	350	20	7,000
Squash, summer	90	4,000	1	4,000
Squash, winter	90	5,000	1	5,000
Swede	15	400	30	12,000
Swiss chard	20	350	20	7,000
Tomatoes	60	6,000	2	12,000
Turnips	15	150	50	7,500

Troubleshooting

Your garden is always going to be at risk of attack by pests and diseases but you can mitigate any damage by taking preventative measures, as well as improving soil and plant health. The small size of the self-sufficiency garden makes spotting the most common pest and disease issues easy. Over the following pages, I outline strategies for keeping on top of them.

PESTS

I would argue that limited numbers of common pests are no bad thing because they attract beneficial insects. These are not only vital for pollinating garden crops but they also feed on pests, which maintains a healthy, natural balance.

Slugs

Of the two most effective ways to combat slugs, the simplest is to go out on warm humid nights with a torch and bucket, then pick them off by hand. The second involves buying nematodes – tiny parasitic creatures that kill slugs. Applying them to your soil in early spring will massively reduce slug numbers for up to six weeks and minimize seedling losses.

Cabbage white caterpillars

These larvae can decimate brassicas but covering the crop with netting doesn't always stop butterflies laying their eggs through it. I don't net brassicas and prefer to check the plants two or three times a week, then pick off any caterpillars.

Aphids and blackfly

These sap-sucking insects often damage the growing tips of plants. Runner beans and field beans are targeted by blackfly, while greenfly prefer tomatoes and leafy green crops. Dislodge them with a jet of water and then spray with diluted plant-based washing-up liquid (2–3 tsp of liquid diluted in 300ml/10fl oz of water). This will kill any remaining pests without harming beneficial insects.

Birds

Pigeons like to feed on brassica leaves but garden birds, such as blackbirds, are more interested in soft fruit. The only effective strategy against birds is to net your crops, but always check nets daily to ensure a bird hasn't got accidentally tangled up in them.

DISEASES

No garden is immune to disease-causing microbes, which are carried in the air or in water. The single most effective strategy is to choose disease-resistant crop varieties, but also take preventative action by boosting the health of your plants with homemade amendments (see p208).

Blight
Affecting both tomatoes and potatoes, this fungal disease strikes in warm, humid conditions and can wipe out an entire crop. Grow blight-resistant varieties when possible, avoid watering foliage, and always ensure good airflow around tomato plants.

Powdery mildew
Like blight, this disease thrives in humid conditions and tends to affect squash, although peas can also suffer. Remove excess squash foliage later in the season, and spray both sides of remaining leaves with diluted LAB (see p208) every two weeks.

Rust
This aptly named orange fungus predominantly targets fava beans and alliums. It may look unsightly but isn't as fast-acting as blight, so I recommend you simply remove any excessively rusted plants. Apply LAB (see p208) to affected leek stems in late summer/early autumn and the rust should disappear when colder weather arrives.

CROP ROTATION

Crop rotation is a fairly complex technique for improving soil and garden health by growing groups of similar crops in a different position next season. They won't return to their original spot for another three or four years, which helps to stop disease build-up in the soil. The small size and high productivity of the self-sufficient garden make crop rotation impractical: most areas will grow two or more different crops, rather than one particular group, over a single season. I focus instead on improving soil health, as well as on attracting beneficial insects.

FLOWERS FOR POLLINATORS

Grow their favourite plants and you'll soon have your own private army of critters, from bees to butterflies, to pollinate your crops as well as kill pests. Once you've attracted the adults they will reproduce, and their larvae – especially those of hoverflies, lacewings, and ladybirds – will then eat amazing numbers of pests. I recommend growing as many of the following herbs and flowers as you can fit in.

Fennel, dill and coriander
The leaves of these three annual herbs will enhance your cooking and their flowers always attract beneficial insects. Let some of your crop run to seed then use seeds in cooking, keeping some for sowing.

Calendula and marigolds
These cheerful orange flowers are insect magnets and really brighten up the garden. Calendula petals also taste good in salads.

Thyme, marjoram, and mint
The tiny flowers of these aromatic perennial herbs are loved by pollinating insects.

Yarrow
Although this plant isn't edible, it's easy to grow and the flat heads attract a wide variety of beneficial insects.

Nettles
Allow a patch to grow in a corner to attract aphids away from your crops. Ladybird larvae will find and eat these pests, and nettles are also the food source of some butterfly larvae.

The Hungry Gap

This gardening term describes the lean period between the end of winter harvests and before summer's abundance – roughly from early April to mid-June. The range of outdoor crops may well be limited, but given the variety of produce growing undercover in the self-sufficiency garden, plus freezer and store cupboard supplies, you shouldn't go hungry.

KEY OUTDOOR HARVESTS

Leek Choose late-bolting varieties for harvesting right up until May (pictured left).

Rhubarb Pick delicious stems throughout the hungry gap (pictured bottom left).

Purple sprouting broccoli Cut tender spears April–May.

Spring cabbage Harvest leaves from April; smaller heads in May and June.

Garlic Harvest green garlic from mid-May onwards and mature bulbs in late June (pictured opposite, third).

Chard Overwintered plants will provide fresh leaves in April and May before running to seed.

Napa cabbage Cut large heads from mid- to late May.

Kale Pick flower shoots from April and into May

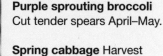

KEY UNDERCOVER HARVESTS (HOOP BEDS AND POLYTUNNEL)

New potatoes* Plant out seed potatoes in February for harvesting from late May onwards (pictured bottom).

Cauliflower* Early February sowings of fast-maturing varieties will yield heads around the start of June (pictured top).

Pak choi* February-sown crops can produce crunchy leaves in as little as six weeks.

Peas* Sow peas in early February to harvest pods from late May.

KEY HOT BED HARVESTS

Salad leaves* February sowings will ensure you are self-sufficient in salad from April onwards.

Carrots and beetroot* Sow in February and enjoy delicious roots from mid-May.

Spring onions Pick from early May to add flavour to salads and leafy greens.

KEY STORAGE YIELDS

Tomatoes Once frozen tomatoes last for months, giving you a taste of summer in early spring.

Onions Cured, homegrown onions should see you through the hungry gap (pictured left, second).

Winter squash Properly cured winter varieties, such as 'Blue Hubbard', will keep for at least six months.

Note on timings*
Having started the self-sufficiency garden in March, I recommended sowing the crops marked* in that month. However, in your second season, once your set-up is working well and provided you have undercover growing space, you could start off all these crops a month earlier.

In the Kitchen

30

Kitchen Overview

Welcome to the kitchen, where produce from the garden is prepped, preserved, and stored so you can eat it all year round. Learn how to unlock the very best flavour and nutrition, process bulk harvests, and plan ahead so you can enjoy homegrown food during the lean months. By using simple techniques I learned in restaurants, you'll discover how to process and cook food in a way that balances efficiency with enjoyment. This isn't about fine dining; it's about celebrating the food you've grown and turning it into the easiest, tastiest meals.

APPROACH

In the following pages, there are many delicious recipes to try, starting with crops you are most likely to be self-sufficient in. Beginning with simple salads and soups, we'll move on to curries, condiments, preserves, purées, pastries, fermentation, sweets, and drinks. But first I'd like to start with the basics and provide a solid foundation that you can build on. Then you can get creative with meals in your own kitchen.

EQUIPMENT

Every recipe in this section of the book requires only basic equipment and the bare minimum you'll need is a couple of large, ovenproof stainless-steel or cast-iron saucepans, a knife, and a chopping board. I also recommend a stick blender or food processor – a great time-saving device for making purées and pesto. I've grouped kitchen equipment into two lists: the first comprises the up-front kit you'll need to get started; the second forms the ideal kitchen set-up and includes specialist kit such as a dehydrator as well as a whiteboard to keep track of your stores.

Basic kit
> Chef's knife, 20–25cm (8–10in)
> Large chopping board
> Stick blender or food processor
> Large frying pan
> Large saucepan

- ❯ 2 large baking trays
- ❯ 5 x 1 litre (1¾ pint) clip-top glass jars
- ❯ 5 x 5 litre (8¾ pint) clip-top glass jars
- ❯ Roll of baking parchment

Ideal kit

- ❯ Chest freezer
- ❯ 20 x 25cm (10in) freezer-proof, airtight containers
- ❯ 10–15 stackable mushroom trays (sourced from a local shop/online)
- ❯ Small whiteboard and whiteboard pens
- ❯ Dehydrator (for drying fresh produce)
- ❯ Upright fridge
- ❯ Set of shelves (for curing/fermentation/bulk storage)
- ❯ Pestle and mortar
- ❯ pH meter

Store cupboard

This is where I keep the homemade produce that can be stored at room temperature, such as flavoured vinegar, oils, chutneys, and ketchup. It also contains staples such as rice, grains, and pasta that have a long shelf life and can be bought in bulk to lower the cost.

- ❯ 5 litres (8¾ pints) olive oil
- ❯ 1 litre (1¾ pints) vinegar (cider or white wine)

- ❯ 1 litre (1¾ pints) dark vinegar (balsamic or red wine)
- ❯ 1 litre (1¾ pints) soy sauce
- ❯ 500g (1lb 2oz) sea salt
- ❯ 10kg (22lb) rice
- ❯ 10kg (22lb) rolled oats
- ❯ 10kg (22lb) pasta
- ❯ 10kg (22lb) legumes, such as red lentils
- ❯ Selection of canned beans, such as kidney

PREP

Good prep is the key to saving time as well as limiting waste in the kitchen. The following tips hold true for most prep, unless a recipe states otherwise.

- ❯ Don't bother peeling your veg. The skins hold a lot of flavour as well as nutrients.
- ❯ Always wash muddy veg in warm, not cold, water. It's quicker and easier.
- ❯ Dicing means 1cm (½in) cubes; chopped ingredients are roughly 1–2cm (½–¾in) long.
- ❯ When using a garlic press, don't peel the cloves first because it's easier to remove the skin afterwards, and makes cleaning much quicker.

- ❯ Leave the root end of an onion intact. It holds the layers together, making chopping or dicing easier.
- ❯ Blend spare greens and veg tops into pesto, then freeze for quick pasta sauces and dressings.
- ❯ Bulk process a cleared crop, such as tomatoes, into purée or soups and freeze. These take up little freezer space and will last for 6–8 months.
- ❯ Use a pH meter to check food is safe to eat when fermenting produce.

FREEZE

Below are my tips for successful freezing:

- ❯ Freeze smaller quantities of individual crops soon after harvesting.
- ❯ Always portion (I tend to use single or double portions) before you freeze food.
- ❯ When labelling frozen food, always stick the label where it will be visible when stacked.
- ❯ When freezing food in bags, lay the filled bags flat. Once frozen, store them upright (like books on a shelf) to save space.

Flavour

Different types of food can be categorized according to flavour and
these flavours interact in different ways. All you need to do is follow
simple rules around flavour pairings and you'll soon improve the taste
of your homegrown food.

There are five principal
flavour types (see right).
Some, such as sweet
and salty – as in salted
caramel – enhance each
other. Others, such as
sweet and acidic, bring
balance so both become
more palatable. Lemonade
without sugar, for example,
would be far too sour.
Once you understand the
characteristics of each
you can combine flavours
successfully in your cooking.

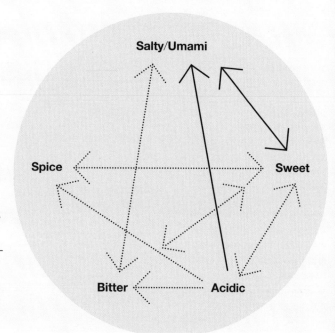

The circle diagram shows flavour
interactions: dark arrows signify
flavours that enhance; dotted arrows
indicate those that balance. Flavours
that are mutually enhancing or
mutually balancing, such as sweet
and spice have two-way arrows.

FLAVOUR TYPES

Salty/Umami; *balances bitterness; enhances sweetness*

Technically, salt and umami are different flavours, but many ingredients high in one are also high in the other. Umami is a savoury flavour we taste when detecting glutamates – naturally occurring amino acids.

Salty

Salt

Anchovies

Hard cheese

Soy sauce

Seaweed

Aged meats

Miso

Kimchi

Fish sauce

Umami

Mushrooms

Tomatoes

Miso

Spice *balances sweet; is balanced by acidic*

As a flavour, spice is the sensation of heat, and dishes with a spicy taste are warming. The term "spice" also refers to aromatic ingredients such as cumin or cinnamon, but these aren't considered "spicy".

Chilli peppers (fresh or dried)

Mustard

Peppercorns

Radishes

Wasabi

Root ginger

Bitter *balances sweet; balanced by salty/umami and acidic*

Used skilfully in small quantities, bitter ingredients can transform a dish, but too much bitterness can be counteracted by sweet, acidic, and umami flavours. Foods with tannin compounds, such as red wine and tea, also belong to this category.

Coffee

Dark chocolate/cocoa

Grapefruit

Beer

Broccoli

Kale

Spinach

Dandelion

Chicory

Okra

Bitter melon

Acidic *balances spice and sweet; enhances salty/umami*

Also called "sour", these ingredients are lively and elevate flavour. Many acidic foods have been fermented.

Citrus fruits

Vinegars (red, white, apple, perry, malt, sherry, balsamic, and rice)

Yoghurt

Sour cream

Goat's or ewe's cheese

Pickled vegetables

Tomatoes

Berries (black/red/white currants)

Sweet *balances acidic, bitter, and spice; enhances salty/umami*

As well as the obvious foods, some root vegetables, such as carrots, taste sweet.

Honey

Sugar

Berries (strawberries and blueberries)

Carrots

Squash

Beetroot

Sweet potatoes

Parsnips

Fat

Although not included in the flavour chart, fats such as cream, yoghurt, crème fraîche, milk, oil, and butter boost the flavour of ingredients and capture aromas that would otherwise be lost from the dish.

FLAVOUR CHART

This chart outlines the key flavours and techniques that are applicable for every ingredient we grew in our self-sufficiency garden. Find the ingredient you wish to use and read to the right of it to learn what its main characteristics are and how best to prepare it. The chart will also help you to decide which flavours might work well when you combine them.

Ingredients (savoury)	Flavour	Raw	Blanched	Steamed	Charred
Aubergine A	Creamy*	—	3 mins (diced, to freeze)	10 mins (1cm thick)	12–16 mins (1cm thic
Beetroot A	Sweet	Tops and grated bulb	20–40 mins (according to size)	30 mins (1cm diced)	8 mins (2cm julienne)
Broad beans B/C	Sweet/mildly bitter)	Very young only	2 mins (to freeze)	3–4mins (podded)	2–3 mins
Broccoli, purple sprouting	Bitter	Yes and leaves, too	2–4 mins	4–5 mins	5–7 mins
Bush/dwarf beans B/C	Sweet/(mildly bitter)	Remove tough end	1 min (to freeze)	3 mins	2–3 mins
Cauliflower A	Sweet	seeSmall leaves	2 mins (head cut into 8ths)	7 mins (florets)	5 mins
Carrot (dwarf) A	Sweet	Tops and grated/ sliced root	2–3 mins (5mm thick slices)	10–12 mins (cut lengthways)	5–6mins (1cm slices)
Celery B/C	Salty	Yes	3 mins	4–5 mins	—
Chard B	Bitter	Shredded/bruised	30 secs– 1 min	1–2 mins	—
Chicory C	Bitter	Yes (as lettuce)	2–3 mins	5–6 mins (whole/ halved)	10 mins (halved, face down)
Chilli (jalapeño) C	Spice	Yes	—	—	3 mins (whole or slice
Cima di rapa B	Bitter (mild)	Yes (leaves)	2–3 mins	3–4 mins	3–4 mins
Climbing French beans B	Sweet	—	3 mins	5 mins	6–7 mins
Courgette B	Creamy*	Yes (when young)	3–5mins (1cm thick)	5 mins (1cm slices)	8 mins (1cm slices)
Cucamelon	Sweet	Yes	—	2 mins (1cm slices)	—
Cucumber C	Sweet	Yes	—	2 mins (1cm slices)	2–3 mins (thin slices)

Flavour notes

A, B, or **C** after the name of the crop indicates this is a bulk ingredient. When building the body of a dish, pick one or two ingredients marked **A**, add one or two marked **B**, but in smaller amounts, and only a small amount of **C**.

Flavours listed as **creamy** and indicated by * are starch rich. This gives them a smooth, creamy (and sometimes sweet) taste.

Tomato is the only acidic ingredient from the garden.

Note on fan ovens

When baking or roasting food in a fan-assisted oven, I would advise lowering the temperature given in the recipe (and in this chart) by 20° C.

...sted (...a drizzle of oil/knob of butter)	Quick pickled	Freeze in portions (generally up to 6 months)	Notes
...mins at 240°C (2cm dice)	—	Blanched/roasted and blended	Blend into a dip with olive oil
...mins at 190°C (whole)	Yes (thinly sliced/grated)	Blanched/roasted and diced (remove leaves)	Reserve leaves for salad or pesto
...mins at 180°C (podded)	Yes (when very young)	Podded, raw or blanched	Pod then skin for smoothest texture
...mins at 200°C (turn halfway ...ugh cooking)	Yes (thinly sliced stem)	Blanched, pat dry	When blanching, add salt to water to keep broccoli green and tasty
...mins at 180°C	Yes (cook first)	Podded, raw or blanched	Blend into pesto with hard cheese, pine nuts, oregano and oil
...ur at 180°C (whole)	Yes (small florets)	Blanched, pat dry	Reserve leaves for salad or fry
...mins at 190°C (whole)	Yes (thinly sliced/grated)	Raw or blanched, chopped (remove leaves)	Reserve leaves for salad or pesto
...25 mins at 180°C	Yes (in chunks)	Raw or blanched, chopped (remove leaves)	Leaves taste pleasantly bitter
...0 mins at 200°C	Yes (remove thick stems)	Blanched, then whole, chopped, or blended	Use leaves and stalks to make kimchi
...ur at 180°C	Yes (halved)	Halved/quartered and blanched, pat dry	Delicious with orange juice and soy sauce
...0 mins at 200°C (whole or sliced)	Yes (thinly sliced)	Raw and whole or puréed	Remove seeds for less heat
...mins at 200°C	Yes (add liquor boiling)	Blanched, then whole, chopped, or blended	
...20 mins at 200°C	—	Blanched	Top and tail before cooking
...mins at 190°C (cut lengthways)	Yes (add liquor hot)	Blanched or roasted and blended	Flowers are also edible
	Yes (takes 24 hrs)	Raw (3 months max)	Add to salads and stir fries just before serving
	Yes (thinly sliced)	Raw (3 months max)	Salt for 10–15 mins before cooking

Ingredients (savoury)	Flavour	Raw	Blanched	Steamed	Charred
Daikon (mooli) A/B	Sweet	Yes (sliced thinly/ add tops)	4–5mins (2cm chunks)	5 mins (very thin slices)	10–15 mins (blanch
Fennel B/C	Sweet	Yes	4 mins (sliced)	15 mins (halved/ quartered)	15 mins (quartered, halfway)
Field beans B/C	Sweet/bitter	Yes (very small only)	2 mins (podded)	4 mins (podded)	10 mins (whole, very young)
Garlic B	Spice	Yes (green garlic stem)	5–6mins	4–5 mins (peeled)	6 mins (leave skin or then peel)
Jerusalem artichoke B	Creamy*	Yes (sliced very thin; see Notes column)	2 mins (thinly sliced)	10 mins (thinly sliced)	10 mins (thinly sliced
Kale (cavolo nero/ curled dwarf) B	Bitter	Yes (see Notes column)	30 secs	1–2 mins	—
Kohlrabi B	Sweet	Yes (grated)	10 mins (1cm slices)	8–12mins (wedges)	10 mins (blanch or s first)
Leek B	Sweet	Yes	30 secs (sliced)	2–3 mins (halved lengthways)	10–15mins (remove outer layer)
Lettuce C	Sweet	Yes	45 secs	1 min	4 mins (halved, brus with oil)
Mustard C	Spice	Yes	10 secs (barely wilted)	20–30 secs (barely wilted)	—
Napa cabbage B	Sweet	Yes (shredded)	1 min (2cm wedges)	4–5 mins (2cm wedges)	10–12 mins (wedges
Onion A	Sweet	Yes (sliced thinly and tops)	—	15–20mins (halved)	25 mins (sliced)
Oriental greens B	Bitter (mild)	Yes	1 min (stems first into water)	3–4 mins (preserves colour)	Until tops wilt
Pak choi B/C	Bitter (mild)	Yes	3 mins (stems first into water)	8–10 mins	10 mins
Pea (mangetout) B/C	Sweet	Yes (use very fresh)	30–40 secs	1–2 mins	2–3 mins
Potato A	Creamy*	—	15–20 mins (3cm cubes)	20 mins (new potatoes)	35–40 mins (wedges
Pumpkin A	Sweet	Yes (leaves)	10–15 mins (3cm cubes, peeled)	25 mins (1cm slices)	20 mins (1cm slices
Radish C	Spice	Yes (sliced thinly and tops)	4–5 mins (2cm chunks)	30 mins (2–3cm chunks)	10–15 mins (blanch f
Rocket C	Spice/bitter	Yes	—	—	—
Runner beans B/C	Sweet/mild bitterness	—	3–4 mins (topped and tailed)	5 mins (topped and tailed)	4–5 mins per side
Shallot A/B	Sweet	Yes (sliced thinly and tops)	—	15–20 mins (halved)	25 mins (sliced)

...sted (... a drizzle of oil/knob of butter)	Quick pickled	Freeze in portions (generally up to 6 months)	Notes
...ins at 180°C (2–3cm chunks)	Yes (thinly sliced)	Blanched, pat dry	Keep radish tops for pestos and leafy salads
...ins at 180°C (quartered)	Yes (thinly sliced)	Halved/quartered then blanched; dry well	Use fronds and flowers as garnishes; seeds are edible
	—	Podded, raw or blanched	No need to pod when harvested very small and sweet
...ins at 200°C (remove base, ...r with foil)	Yes (thinly sliced)	Whole, peeled or puréed; wrap tightly	Enjoy garlic when green as well as cured bulbs
...0 mins at 180°C (roasted ...le/halved)	—	Blanched	Can produce gas when eaten raw
...0 mins at 210°C (finish with ...me oil)	Yes (shredded)	Blanched then whole, chopped, or blended	Remove stem
...ins at 180°C (wedges)	Yes (grated)	Blanched (remove leaves)	Add leaves to salads
...ins at 190°C (whole, remove ...r layer)	Yes (add liquor hot)	Blanched or shredded and sautéd in butter	
...5 mins at 210°C (whole/halved)	Yes	Puréed (thaw before adding to soups)	
	Yes	Puréed (thaw before adding to soups)	Buds and flowers are edible
...ins at 200°C (wedges)	Yes (thinly sliced)	Blanched, pat dry; or made into kimchi	Turn halfway when charring/roasting
...ins at 190°C (skin on)/30mins ...ed)	Yes (thinly sliced)	Raw, chopped or blended	Add to any quick pickle
...mins at 190°C (until wilted)	Yes (remove thick stems)	Blanched, pat dry	Treat like a robust chard
...ins at 220°C (halved)	Yes	Blanched, pat dry	
...ns (add extra oil to crisp up)	Yes	Raw (freshly picked)	Harvest shoots for salads and garnishing
...ins at 190°C (3cm dice/new ...toes halved)	—	Parboiled	Cover chopped potatoes in water to prevent browning
...ur at 190°C (quartered, seeds ...oved)	Yes (thinly sliced)	Peeled and parboiled	Save seeds, clean, then roast as a snack
...ins at 180°C (2–3cm chunks)	Yes	Blanced, pat dry	Keep tops for pesto and add to leafy salads
	Yes	Puréed (thaw before adding to soups)	Blend into pesto and add to cooked dishes for a peppery taste
...20 mins at 220°C (whole)	Yes (cook first)	Blanched	Beans from over-large, stringy pods can be cooked and eaten
...ins at 190°C (skin on)/30mins ...ed)	Yes (thinly sliced)	Raw, chopped or blended	Add to any quick pickle

Ingredients (savoury)	Flavour	Raw	Blanched	Steamed	Charred
Spinach (malabar) B	Sweet	Baby leaves	1–2 mins (according to size)	3 mins	No but will sauté
Squash (winter) A	Sweet	Young leaves	10–15mins (3cm cubes, peeled)	25 mins (2cm cubes)	25 mins (2cm dice)
Spring cabbage B	Sweet	Yes (shredded)	30 secs (shredded)/ 2 mins (wedges)	3 mins (chopped/ shredded)	3 mins (shredded)/ 4–5mins (wedges)
Spring onion C	Spice	Yes	20 secs (whole)	1 min (whole)	2 mins (whole, turne halfway)
Swede A	Sweet	Leafy tops	2 mins (2cm cubes, to freeze)	25 mins (2cm cubes)	5 mins (diced, blanc first)
Tomato A/B	Acidic	Yes	30 secs–1min (whole)	—	3 mins (whole, until blackens)
Tree cabbage B	Sweet	Shredded leaves	1 min	3 mins	2–3 mins (finely shredded)
Turnip A	Sweet	Leafy tops	2 mins (2cm cubes, to freeze)	25 mins (2cm cubes)	3 mins (diced, blanc first)
Wild garlic B/C	Spice/bitter	Yes	1 min	—	4 mins

Herbs (perennial)	Infuse in oil	Raw (serve raw)	Pesto ingredient	Notes
Chives	Yes (blend)	Yes	Yes	Strong tasting flowers also infuse well
Lemon balm	Yes (blend)	Yes	Yes	Beautiful with roasts. Use leaves only
Lemon verbena	Yes (blend)	Yes	Yes	Pairs well with garlic. Use leaves only
Mint	Yes (blend)	Yes	Yes	
Oregano	Yes (blend)	Yes	Yes	Use leaves only
Rosemary	Yes	Yes	Yes	Use leaves only. Infuse leaves and woody stem in oil
Thyme	Yes	Yes	Yes	Use leaves only. Infuse leaves and woody stem in oil

sted	Quick pickled	Freeze in portions (generally up to 6 months)	Notes
a drizzle of oil/knob of butter)			
	Yes	Blanched, then whole, chopped, or blended	Blend into pesto to add bulk
ins at 190°C (2cm dice)	—	Peeled and parboiled	Winter and summer squash are cooked the same way
ins at 200°C (in wedges)	Yes (shredded)	Blanched, pat dry	Shred excess and turn into sauerkraut
s at 200°C (turned halfway)	Yes (chopped)	Raw then chopped	Leaves add flavour if you don't have bulbs
ins at 200°C (2cm cubes)	Yes (grated)	Blanched, pat dry	Cook as for potatoes
ur at 160°C (halved or whole)	Yes (add liquor hot)	Scalded to remove skin, then whole or puréed	Great on toast with garlic, olive oil, and salt
ins at 210°C (2cm slices)	Yes (2cm slices)	Blanched, pat dry	Wrap leaves round other ingredients before cooking
ins at 200°C (3cm chunks)	Yes (grated)	Blanched, pat dry	Cook as for potatoes
to other roasts 4 mins before ing	Yes	Blended into pesto	Add to other dishes 2 mins before serving

s (al)	Infuse in oil	Raw (serve raw)	Pesto ingredient	Notes
	Yes (blend)	Yes	Yes	
ge	Yes (blend)	Yes	Yes	Flowers taste like cucumber
nder	Yes (blend)	Yes	Yes	Use leaves, flowers, and seeds
	Yes (blend)	Yes	Yes	Use leaves, flowers, and seeds
ey	Yes (blend)	Yes	Yes	Use leaves, flowers, and seeds

Salads

All kinds of homegrown produce can be turned into the freshest, crunchiest salads. Given the wide range of vegetables and herbs you can grow in the garden, these versatile dishes need never be boring.

Healthy, deilcious-tasting salads can be great fun to put together, and the dressing couldn't be simpler: just follow the golden rule (see p164) when mixing oil and vinegar. I'm also sharing techniques for prepping ingredients that will give your salad an extra layer of flavour. Check the flavour chart (see pp156–161) for crops that can be added raw, blanched, or charred, as well as herbs (and flowers) to include for taste and colour.

SALAD TECHNIQUES

Be creative and add interest and texture to salads by adding steamed or charred fresh veg, as well as grains, nuts, and bread.

Raw and chopped
Preserving the freshness and crunch of raw salad ingredients is key. Lettuce, carrots, radish, cabbage, and cucumber are at their best when just-picked and served promptly. Also, don't be tempted to dress your salad too soon before eating as the acid in the vinegar will soften the ingredients and ruin the perfect crunch.

Steamed and blanched
Both these techniques maximize the nutritional content of homegrown produce. To create a makeshift steamer, simply place a sieve over a saucepan of boiling water, add veg, such as climbing beans, and cover with a lid. Blanching involves briefly

plunging veg into salted, boiling water, and then interrupting the process with cold water to preserve their texture, flavour, and colour. By adding salt (1tbsp per 400ml/14fl oz water), we raise the water's mineral content and stop vital nutrients leaching out.

Charred and roasted
When you char veg such as leeks (pictured opposite) and broccoli, it adds depth and smokiness, while on the inside they are lightly steamed. To char, put a cast iron pan on the stove, and when very hot, place veg directly onto it. Leave until the veg are blackened and crispy on the edges, then turn them over and repeat. Oven-roasting ingredients

in oil, including tomatoes, aubergines, and root vegetables, breaks down their sugars and intensifies the flavour. For a little extra crunch in salads, I would recommend roasting kale into crisps.

Quick pickling

Not just a preserving technique, pickling adds interest to veg and provides an acidic and lively hit to dishes. You can batch pickle any of the ingredients listed on the flavour chart by slicing them very thinly (using a mandoline or hand-slicer) and then immersing in a pickling liquor. For roughly every 400–500g (14oz–1lb 2oz) of veg, put 250ml (9fl oz) vinegar, 250ml (9fl oz) water, 100g (3½ oz) sugar and 1 tsp salt in a 1.5-litre (2¾-pint) jar. Flavour the pickle with spices and herbs and put it in the fridge. You can use it after an hour but the veg will taste stronger and be fully pickled after 24–48 hours. The pickle will keep for up to a week.

Special additions

Another way to liven up your salads is to add grains and pulses, such as quinoa, barley, couscous, or mixed, cooked beans. Cheese will boost savouriness while nuts add crunch, and you can also sprinkle over a pinch of one of the spice blends from the curry section (see p170). Adding carbs works well and

I've included a recipe that uses roasted bread. And if you're struggling to feed extra people, you can always bulk out the salad with a tasty cooked pasta, dressed with oil to stop it from drying out. I've grouped the following salad recipes into Summer and Spring to celebrate a handful of my favourite ingredients and showcase a few examples of the wonderful versatility of salad.

Dressing
The best salad dressings consist of just two ingredients and I always use them in the following proportions: one-third vinegar to two-thirds oil. As with all simple recipes, these dressings rely on the quality of their ingredients. From a lively cider vinegar to a bold, fruity balsamic, every vinegar has something different. Strong-tasting ingredients infused in vinegar, such as nasturtium petals or allium flowers, also add a wonderful flavour and a fantastic aroma. Oils, on the other hand, can range from peppery to buttery – even "meadowy" – in flavour. Oils also make excellent carriers for aromatic herbs, including rosemary and thyme.

SUMMER SALADS

Make the most of plentiful summer vegetables with these two great-tasting, warm-weather salads.

Tomato and bread

This salad, which can be eaten hot or cold, is perfect for sharing. The flavour is acidic, deeply savoury, and it is very "moreish"

Serves 2

4 thick slices of bread

5 tbsp olive oil

Salt and pepper to taste

3 fresh sprigs of thyme

8–9 large tomatoes

2 garlic cloves, sliced thinly

1 tbsp balsamic vinegar

Optional

Fresh basil

1. Preheat the oven to 180°C (350°F). Cut the bread into 2cm (¾in) cubes, scatter them over a baking tray and drizzle with the olive oil. Season with salt and pepper, then place the sprigs of thyme on top and roast for 25 minutes or until the bread is dried and crunchy.

2. Add the tomatoes to the bread on the tray and lightly crush them with a wooden spoon to split the skins. Add the sliced garlic, return to the tray to the oven and turn it up to 200°C (400°F). Roast for another 20 minutes then serve in a bowl with a drizzle of balsamic vinegar and torn fresh basil.

Quick pickled cucumber and mushrooms
A clean, acidic, sweet salad that's best served cold as a side dish. It's ideal for using up gluts of cucumber.

Serves 2

200ml (7fl oz) cold water

Pinch of salt

½ tsp green coriander seeds

80g (2¾oz) raw cane sugar

200ml (7fl oz) cider vinegar

1 large cucumber

200g (7oz) shiitake mushrooms

1 tsp toasted sesame oil

1 tsp sesame seeds

6–7 pea shoots

1. Gently heat the water, salt, coriander seeds, sugar, and vinegar in a saucepan until the salt and sugar are fully dissolved. Now remove from the heat and allow the liquid to cool while you prep the other ingredients.

2. Using a sharp knife or mandoline, thinly slice the cucumber and mushrooms into an airtight container. Pour over the pickling liquor, cover with a lid, and leave in the fridge for 1–3 hours before eating.

3. Serve the salad dressed with the sesame oil and seeds, and garnish with pea shoots.

SPRING SALAD

Bring out the flavour of your freshly dug new potatoes in this delicious, creamy salad (pictured below).

Steamed potato, sour cream, and spring onion

Spring onion adds a lovely, fresh taste to this salad, but you can use chives and wild garlic also works well.

Serves 2 generously

800g (1¾lb) small or new potatoes, halved

3 fresh rosemary sprigs

100ml (3½fl oz) sour cream

1tsp wholegrain mustard

3 spring onions, finely sliced

2 tbsp peppery olive oil

Salt and pepper to taste

1. Steam the potatoes and rosemary over 500ml (16fl oz) of boiling water for 12–15 minutes until tender.

2. Remove the rosemary and allow the potatoes to cool in a bowl for 20 minutes.

3. Mix the cream, mustard, and onion, then pour over the potatoes. Drizzle with olive oil before serving.

Soups

Almost any homegrown produce can be turned into nourishing soup with maximum flavour. It's a great way to use up leftovers or when you clear a crop, such as tomatoes. Soup is also easily batch processed for the freezer, where it can be stored for up to six months.

My approach to soup making follows five easy steps that are applicable to every ingredient from the garden. The soups are designed to be rustic and flavoursome, so I often leave the skins on vegetables. Once you're familiar with these steps, consult the flavour chart (see pp156–161) and enjoy experimenting with soup creations.

1. Start with aromatics
These are the foundation of any soup and can include chopped onion, garlic, celery (pictured left), carrot, and bell pepper. Choose two or three and sauté gently in oil or butter for 20 minutes to release their flavour. If you want to use whole spices or

perennial herbs, such as rosemary and thyme, add them at this stage.

2. Deglaze

This crucial step elevates the flavour of a dish. Add a splash of vinegar or wine to the sautéed ingredients when cooked, then allow the liquid to reduce. The mix will quickly evaporate, becoming sticky and concentrated. I use red wine or red wine vinegar in beetroot soup. Choose white wine or cider vinegar to deglaze in soups with creamy or white ingredients.

3. Add bulk ingredients and stock

Giving the soup its principal flavour, bulk ingredients tend to be abundant crops, including tomatoes, leeks, and potatoes. Grains and pulses can also be added at this stage to increase volume and nutrition. Pick one to three bulk ingredients then add enough stock to cover and put a lid on the pan. The best stocks are homemade, create zero waste, and can be made by simmering your vegetable scraps for two hours with aromatic ingredients, water, and salt. Alternatively, buy vegetable stock powder.

4. Inject freshness

From leafy herbs to chard and sugarsnap peas, many fresh ingredients are highly sensitive to temperature.

Always add them just a minute or two before serving (either before or after blending) and then let the residual heat of the soup unlock their flavour.

5. Add a final flourish

Once you've identified the overall flavour of the soup, it's time to add a second, complementary one to make the soup truly shine. A dash of cream will balance an acidic tomato soup, while soft cheese counteracts any bitterness from brassicas, such as kale.

RECIPES

The following recipes will make around 15 portions – enough for batch freezing.

Leek and potato

A really flavoursome winter staple with just enough white wine to enhance the miso.

2 onions

1 carrot, chopped

2 celery stalks, chopped

1 tbsp salted butter

90ml (3fl oz) white wine

2 garlic cloves, crushed

2kg (4½lbs) potatoes, diced

2 turnips or ½ swede, diced

2 tbsp wholegrain mustard

2 tsp sweet white miso

Salt and black pepper

Vegetable stock

2 leeks (including green parts), finely chopped

Optional

Chopped parsley added just before or after blending

Sauté the chopped aromatics (onions, carrot, celery) in butter for 20 minutes, then add the wine and garlic. When the wine has reduced, add the remaining ingredients except for the leeks. Cover with stock and simmer until the potatoes are soft. Now add the leeks, season, and blend the soup immediately to preserve its vivid colour.

Tomato

A soup with rich acid and umami flavours (pictured right). Summer vegetables, such as aubergines or courgettes, work well with the tomatoes, and the soup can be enjoyed cold.

2 onions

2 carrots, chopped

2 bell peppers, de-seeded)
2 tbsp olive oil

100ml (3½fl oz) red wine vinegar

3kg (6½lbs) fresh tomatoes (skins left on)

3 garlic cloves, crushed

2 tsp smoked paprika

1–2 fresh chillies (include seeds for more heat)

2 tbsp soy sauce

Black pepper

Vegetable stock

To serve

Splash of single cream

Fresh basil

Optional

500g (1lb 2oz) summer vegetables, such as aubergine and courgettes

500g (1lb 2oz) red lentils

Fresh basil, thyme, or rosemary

Sauté the onions, carrots, and peppers in oil for 20 minutes then deglaze with the vinegar, letting the mix reduce until sticky. Add the tomatoes whole with the garlic and remaining ingredients (including any of the options). Pour in enough stock to cover then simmer for 25–30 minutes. Blend or leave chunky and serve with cream or fresh basil.

TIP

To make croutons for soup, chop stale bread into small pieces, toss in oil, salt, and thyme, and roast in the oven. You can also blend croutons into tomato soup for extra creaminess.

Udon broth

The vinegar, soy, and Worcestershire sauce mix in this summer soup is also ideal for flavouring stir fries.

900g (10oz) mushrooms, quartered

2 tbsp rapeseed oil

3 onions

6 carrots, chopped

6 celery stalks

3 tbsp soy sauce

5 tbsp cider vinegar

2.5cm (1in) piece ginger root, peeled and thinly sliced

3.5 litres (6 pints) vegetable stock

2 courgettes (plus flowers), chopped

90g (3oz) sugarsnap peas

Handful of oriental greens

3 tbsp Worcestershire sauce

To serve

2–3 tbsp kimchi

2 radishes, thinly sliced

2 spring onions, thinly sliced

150g (5oz) udon noodles per person (or boiled potato, cubed)

Optional

1 tbsp honey

Flash fry the mushrooms whole in hot oil until golden, then reduce the heat and add the onion, carrots, and celery, plus the soy sauce, vinegar, ginger root. Add the stock once the sauce has reduced. Simmer for 30 minutes then add the remaining ingredients, including the honey if using. After 5 more minutes, pour into bowls, add the kimchi, and garnish with the sliced radishes and spring onions.

Brassica and goat's cheese
This winter soup perfectly balances the bitterness of plentiful brassicas with a soft cheese. In summer, you could substitute bolted lettuces, which will have lost their sweetness.

2 onions, chopped

2 carrots, chopped

3 celery stalks

30g (1oz) salted butter

200ml (7fl oz) white wine

2 large potatoes, diced

3 garlic cloves, crushed

2 tbsp wholegrain mustard

3.5 litres (6 pints) vegetable stock

150g (5½oz) French beans

2kg (4½lb) of any brassica leaves, chopped

350g (12oz) soft goat's cheese

Salt and black pepper

Sauté the onions, carrots, and celery in butter then deglaze with white wine. Add the diced potatoes, garlic, mustard, and stock, and simmer for 30 minutes. Now add the beans, chopped brassica leaves, and goat's cheese. Season to taste, then blend until smooth.

Curries

Adding spices to classic garden vegetables injects interest, colour, and excitement into your cooking. To clarify, by "spice" I mean fragrance, as opposed to heat. Spices have a wealth of aromatic compounds that smell and taste fantastic, adding complexity to even the simplest dish.

SPICE BLENDS

All these spice blends are highly versatile and can be added to soups, sauces, condiments, and pickles. My recipes are for bulk quantities to save time, and each one makes enough to fill a 300g (10oz) glass jar. Make sure the jar has an airtight lid and store out of direct sunlight. For the best flavour, use within six months, although the blends will last for years. Buy whole spices and grind them before storing and using.

All-purpose blend
Savoury, balanced, and floral, this solid all-rounder works beautifully in any type of curry and gives a nice boost to soups. The all-purpose blend (pictured below, bottom right) also makes a great BBQ rub: sprinkle onto ingredients and rub in well ahead of cooking.

4 tbsp paprika (sweet or smoked)

3 tbsp coriander seeds

3 tbsp cumin seeds

2 tbsp curry powder (mild or hot)

2 tbsp ground turmeric

1 tsp garam masala

1 tsp freshly ground black pepper

1tsp chilli powder

1tsp onion powder

1tsp garlic flakes

Panch phoron (puran)
Fenugreek, nigella, and fennel give this pungent blend (pictured opposite, top left) an earthy, bitter taste. It is a feature of classic Bengali dishes, such as saag aloo. Grind the seeds in a pestle and mortar before using.

4 tbsp cumin seeds

4 tbsp yellow mustard seeds

4 tbsp fennel seeds

4 tbsp nigella seeds

2 tbsp fenugreek seeds*

*If you find the blend too bitter, halve the amount of fenugreek.

Baharat
A Middle Eastern blend with a smoky, fruity, sweet taste: perfect in tomato dishes, with cooked meats, and added to hummus. Crack the cardamom pods to remove the seeds and pound them with the cloves in a pestle and mortar before mixing with the other spices.

4 tbsp smoked paprika

4 tbsp ground cumin

2 tbsp ground black pepper

2 tbsp ground coriander

1 tbsp grated nutmeg

1 tbsp ground cinnamon

2 tsp allspice powder

1 tsp cardamom pods

1 tsp cloves

Shichimi togarashi
My twist on this classic Japanese blend releases nutty, warming, and citrus aromas. First toast the sesame seeds in the oven at 180°C (350°F) for 10 minutes and either dry the orange peel naturally (takes 2–3 weeks), or in the oven at 140°C (275°F) for 1 hour.

Coarsely grind all the ingredients in a pestle and mortar, then use in cooking or sprinkle on cooked dishes. It also tastes great on popcorn.

4 tbsp sesame seeds

Dried peel from 1 orange

2 tbsp chilli flakes

2 tbsp dried seaweed (dulse or nori)

3 tsp black peppercorns

1 tbsp poppy seeds

1 tsp ground ginger

CURRY SAUCES

Using a combination of the spice blends, I'm sharing two curry sauce recipes to suit both summer and winter crops from the garden.

Summer tomato curry sauce

Featuring three of the spice blends, plus fresh tomatoes and spiced yoghurt, this sauce goes well with a mix of garden veg. For this quantity of sauce, I suggest adding 400g (14oz) root veg, 300g (10oz) mushrooms or green beans, and 250g (9oz) of leafy greens.

Serves 3–4

2 tsp panch phoron

3 garlic cloves, crushed

200ml (7fl oz) natural yoghurt

3 tbsp rapeseed oil

1 onion, diced

2 garlic cloves, crushed

2 tbsp butter

1 tbsp all-purpose spice blend

1 tsp baharat

100ml (3½fl oz) stock/2water

400g (14oz) tomatoes, chopped

1 tsp sea salt

1. Mix the panch phoron and 3 garlic cloves into the yoghurt. Leave in the fridge for 1 hour (3 days max).

2. Put 1 tbsp of the oil in a large frying pan on a medium heat and sauté the onion until translucent, then add the 2 garlic cloves and cook for a further 3 minutes.

3. Add the butter to the pan and fry the all-purpose and baharat spice blends in it for 30–40 seconds so they become highly fragrant. Now add the stock, tomatoes, and salt, and cook for another 30 minutes until the sauce has thickened.

4. Add your chosen veg to the sauce and simmer until all the vegetables are tender.

5. Serve with naan, rice, and a bowl of the spiced yoghurt on the side.

Winter coconut curry sauce

Celebrating homegrown winter produce, this sauce (pictured right) is fantastic with pumpkin, winter greens, and canned beans. The shichimi togarashi really comes to life when infused in the rich coconut. For this quantity of sauce, I'd use 600g (1lb 5oz) in total of mixed greens, starchy vegetables, and beans.

Serves 3–4

1 onion, diced

2 garlic cloves, crushed

1 tbsp olive oil

Pinch of salt and freshly ground pepper

1 tsp all-purpose spice blend

1 tsp soy sauce

1 tsp yuzu citrus seasoning or lemon juice

150ml (5fl oz) stock or water

400ml (14fl oz) coconut milk

2.5cm (1in) fresh ginger, peeled and grated

2 tbsp shichimi togarashi

1 tsp wholegrain mustard

1. Sauté the onion and garlic in the olive oil over a medium to low heat until translucent. Season with salt and pepper.

2. Add the all-purpose spice blend and fry gently for 1 minute before adding the soy sauce and yuzu/lemon juice. Let the liquid reduce for a minute until sticky.

3. Now add the stock and coconut milk, along with the remaining ingredients. Bring to a simmer and cook for 12 minutes.

4. Add your chosen veg to the sauce and simmer until all the vegetables are tender.

5. Top with a pinch of shichimi and serve with rice.

Condiments

Encompassing sauces, dips, and purées, condiments are the cook's secret ingredients and they also make great side dishes. From ketchup to pesto, the following recipes can be adapted to suit a range of garden veg and herbs, and most can be frozen successfully.

Ketchup

Any root veg or aromatics that you have in abundance. will work in this recipe for ketchup (pictured left). It's a fantastic way to enjoy them out of season and will keep for six months. To turn it into a BBQ sauce, add 3 tbsp each of the all-purpose spice blend and baharat (see pp170–171) during cooking.

Makes 3.5 litres (6 pints)

900g (2lb) vegetables and leafy greens

2kg (4½lb) tomatoes

1 onion, chopped

5 garlic cloves, minced

700ml (1¼ pints) water

2 fresh chillies

2 tbsp smoked paprika

4 cloves, ground

2 tbsp soy sauce

1 tbsp salt

1 tsp freshly ground black pepper

150g (5½oz) demerara sugar

400ml (14fl oz) vinegar: red wine/malt/sherry

Wash and prepare your chosen veg and place them in a large saucepan. Add all the other ingredients except for the sugar and vinegar. Bring to a boil, then simmer until the volume has reduced by half. Blend the resulting sauce in a food processor until smooth, then pass

haricot beans

400g (14oz) raw beetroot/carrot, grated or

270g (9½oz) young spinach or wild garlic leaves

200g (7oz) light tahini

Juice of 2 lemons

4 garlic cloves, peeled

2 tsp salt

60ml (2fl oz) olive oil

through a fine sieve and return it to the saucepan. Now add the vinegar and sugar and bring to a simmer until the sauce is glossy (10–15 minutes). While still piping hot, pour into sterilized bottles. When cool, store for up to six months. Once opened, refrigerate and use within six weeks.

Pesto
In this popular pasta sauce (pictured above), soft herbs are blended with spices and garlic then mixed with hard cheese or toasted nuts, salt, and olive oil. Basil is the classic ingredient but rocket, young kale, carrot tops, parsley, or coriander make good substitutes.

90g (3oz) grated parmesan/toasted hazelnuts

100g (3½oz) soft herbs

50g (1¾oz) leafy greens

2 tsp wholegrain mustard

3 garlic cloves, peeled

250ml (9fl oz) olive oil

Juice of a lemon

Pinch of salt (if using hazelnuts)

Toast the hazelnuts in a pan over a medium heat for 10 minutes (if substituting for cheese). Put them into a food processor with all the other ingredients and blend. Transfer the pesto to an airtight container and store in the fridge for a week, or freeze for up to six months. I like to make the pesto a day ahead to allow the flavours to develop.

Dip
This recipe is loosely based on hummus, with the option of adding either root veg or leafy greens for texture and flavour. It can be frozen for up to six months.

2 tbsp cumin seeds

800g (1¾lb) cooked chickpeas/butter beans/

Toast the cumin seeds in a pan until fragrant and set aside, then blend everything else except the oil in a food processor. Once smooth, add the toasted seeds and drizzle in the oil while keeping the motor running. Store in the fridge, in an airtight container or jar, for up to a week.

Purée
Dice then simmer any starchy vegetable, or a mix of two or three, in boiling salted water until soft. Drain then blend until smooth with your chosen herbs. Puréed squash, for example, tastes great paired with rosemary. Season to taste and loosen with water, cream, or melted butter until you're happy with the consistency. If, on the other hand, the purée is too loose, return it to a gentle heat and reduce until thickened. Purées freeze well for up to six months.

Easy Pastry

This hot-water crust pastry couldn't be simpler and the pies, tarts, and pasties you make can be filled with fresh garden produce, as well as leftovers. Pastry also freezes well and can be stored for up to six months, so it makes sense to save time and batch cook for the freezer.

Makes 1 medium pie, 2 tarts, or 4 pasties

150ml (5fl oz) water

130g (4½ oz) butter

380g (13oz) plain flour plus extra for dusting

PInch of salt

Optional
½ tsp white vinegar to maintain freshness

1. Put the water and butter into a small saucepan and then heat gently until the butter has melted.

2. Meanwhile, put the flour and salt into a bowl. Add the butter cut into small pieces and rub it in with your fingers.

3. Turn up the heat and when the liquid reaches a rolling boil, pour it straight into the bowl and mix with a spoon until well combined.

4. Dust a work surface lightly with flour and tip the pastry onto it. As soon as it's cool enough to handle, knead lightly until all the dry flour is incorporated.

5. Roll out the pastry to a thickness of 5mm (¼in) and shape to fit your tins. Work quickly: the pastry is easier to handle when still warm.

6. For pasties, make a circle of around 23cm (9in) and place the filling in the middle of the pastry. Brush the edge of half the pastry circle with

water or milk, then bring it up to meet the other half, crimping the edge to seal it. **For pies** (pictured opposite), add the filling then brush around the edge with water or milk before placing the pastry lid on top. Crimp to seal. **For tarts and quiches**, use a ratio of 3 eggs to 500ml (16fl oz) cream together with your chosen garden veg and/or cheese.

7. Set the oven to 190°C (375°F) then brush the tops of the pies or pasties with milk or with egg wash (2 tbsp cold water mixed with an egg yolk). Bake individual pasties or small pies (10cm/4in) for 40 minutes. A large pie (23cm/9in), such as the

one pictured above, will take around 50 minutes.

For additional flavour, sprinkle the tops of pies with sesame seeds, cracked peppercorns, grated cheese, or smoked paprika before you bake them.

Batch cooking and freezing
When batch cooking for the freezer, I recommend you brush the filled, unbaked pies or pasties with egg wash or milk to stop the pastry from drying out or cracking. Now lay a piece of baking parchment on top of each and stack them one on top of the other in an airtight container. The parchment will stop them sticking together so they are easier to take apart while still frozen. To freeze tarts and quiches bake them first and freeze in portions once cooled. To cook from frozen, place pies, pasties, and quiche portions in airtight containers, then defrost in the fridge for 12 hours. Bake as for fresh pies. For a super-quick meal, cook pies or pasties straight from the freezer. Bake at 190°C (375°F) for 45 minutes.

Tip
For a quick and easy pie filling, mix 4 parts lightly steamed vegetables/cooked beans/mushrooms with 1 part purée/ketchup/gravy/ grated cheese/leftover curry.

No-Knead Focaccia

Fresh, homemade bread tastes fantastic and fills the kitchen with a wonderful aroma. Even better, this simple and reliable method of making focaccia skips the most time-consuming part – kneading the dough – making it easier to fit breadmaking into a busy day.

When you make your own bread, you know exactly what's gone into it – unlike expensive shop-bought loaves that often contain preservatives and anti-caking agents. My no-knead version of Italian focaccia is packed with natural flavour and includes fresh summer vegetables. Add your choice of sliced garden veg and perhaps include nuts or seeds for added texture.

**Makes 1 large tray or
2 smaller trays**

800g (1¾lb) strong bread flour (white or wholemeal)

640ml (1.1 pints) cold water

1½ tsp sea salt

1 tsp dried yeast

1. Measure out then mix all the ingredients together in a large bowl, cover, and leave in the fridge for a minimum of 6 hours (use within 24 hours).

2. One hour before you're ready to bake, take the bowl out of the fridge and loosen the dough from all the way round the edge by inserting a rubber spatula, folding the dough over as you go (pictured right, above). If the dough is too stiff, let it warm for 15 minutes before folding. Now leave the dough for 30 minutes.

3. Next, prepare your baking tray with a light drizzle of oil and lift the dough onto it. To do this, hook both hands

under the dough on either side and move them apart over the tray, allowing the weight to stretch the dough, which will hang down. Now neaten and shape the dough by pushing it towards the corners of the tray, then oil the top and let it rest for another 20–30 minutes.

4. Lightly press the dough with your finger and if it bounces back by half the depth of the indentation, then it's ready to bake.

5. Oil your hands and press your fingers deep into the dough all over to create large bubbles and creases. Now push your chosen veg into the creases along with a pinch of salt and extra oil (pictured below). Whole cherry tomatoes, slices of tomato, onion, peppers, or courgettes all work well.

6. Set the oven to 230°C (450°F), and place a deep baking tray on the bottom. Put the focaccia into the preheated oven, and pour 90ml (3fl oz) of water into the deep baking tray underneath it to create steam.

7. After 30 minutes the loaf should be well risen and done. Now turn the oven off, and prop the door slightly ajar. Giving the loaf a further 20 minutes will "cure" it and create a satisfying crust (see below, right).

Tip
When using frozen bread, including this vegetable focaccia, first soak it in cold water and squeeze lightly.

Then bake the bread in a preheated oven for 15 minutes at 180°C (350°F). It will taste as good as freshly baked.

One-Tray Bakes

Making tempting savoury and sweet bakes from garden produce is surprisingly easy. All you need is a mixing bowl and a roasting tin or deep baking tray. I've included suggestions rather than specific recipes for the savoury bakes, and recommend making large quantities so you can portion and freeze them once cooked.

SAVOURY

Tray bakes are the simplest way to cook multiple meals from many ingredients.

Pasta bake

This is one of the most versatile dishes to make with garden produce, whatever the season. Mix fresh or tinned tomatoes with al dente pasta (check the pack for timing) and diced veg in the tray, then pour in enough stock to almost cover. Try adding a teaspoon of the spice blends (see p170), vinegar, or seasoning from the store cupboard, and top with grated cheese. Bake for 25 minutes at 190°C (375°F).

Potato hash

Whenever I've got the oven on at 180°C (350°F), I'll pop a few potatoes on the bottom shelf to bake for 1½ hours, then store them in the fridge (three days) or freezer (six months). To make hash, sauté onion, garlic, leeks, or spring onion in butter with seasoning while you remove the skin from the potatoes and roughly chop the flesh. Mix everything together, add veg (either finely diced or grated), and squash it all into the tray. Bake for 15 minutes at 200°C (400°F), then crack an egg on top of the hash and return to the oven to bake for another 10–15 minutes. Garnish with herbs or sprinkle spice on top.

Casserole

Delicious, hearty casseroles are one-dish wonders. Pick something savoury, such as mushrooms or sausage, and fry with a drizzle of oil until sticky and browned. Add base aromatics, fry for a couple of minutes, then deglaze with wine, vinegar, or Worcestershire sauce. Transfer everything to the baking tray, adding as many diced garden veg as you can fit in, followed by some chopped fresh or tinned tomatoes and stock to cover. Put a sheet of foil over the tray and bake at 160°C (320°F) for 2 hours, then uncover and give it another 30 minutes at 180°C (350°F) to thicken.

Tip
For a really filling casserole, make dumplings from flour, butter, and water. Flavour with herbs and place on the top of the uncovered casserole for the last 30 minutes of cooking.

SWEET

Homegrown ingredients also make the best sweet treats, including carrot, beetroot or courgette

Brownies and blondies
Incorporate grated vegetables and berries into this deliciously fudgy chocolate brownie. Or try the briliant blondie variation (pictured right). Both can be frozen for 6–8 months.

Makes 12 portions

170ml (5½fl oz) olive oil

400g (14oz) golden icing sugar

180ml (6fl oz) milk or oat milk

1 tsp salt

230g (8oz) plain flour

½ tsp baking powder

90g (3oz) cocoa powder (omit for blondie)

180g (6oz) dark chocolate (white for blondie), chopped small

100g (3½oz) mixed grated raw beetroot/courgette and berries **or**

100g (3½oz) mixed grated carrot and berries (for blondie)

1tsp vanilla extract (for blondie)

Optional
⅓ tsp each ground nutmeg, cinnamon, and mixed spice for a spiced brownie/blondie.

1. Preheat the oven to 190°C (375°F) and beat the icing sugar and olive oil until it resembles thick butter icing.

2. Add half the milk and stir well before adding the remaining half. Mix again until smooth.

3. In a separate bowl, measure out the remaining ingredients except for the

chocolate, berries, and vegetables, and mix until well combined.

4. Add some of the wet mixture to the dry ingredients and fold in until well incorporated, then add the remainder with the grated vegetables or berries. Do not over mix.

5. Add the chocolate pieces and mix them into the batter.

6. Line a baking tray with baking parchment and pour the batter in, smoothing the top with a spatula. Bake for 25–30 minutes.

7. When cool, transfer the tray to the fridge and leave for an hour to set before cutting the brownies or blondies into portions.

Preserves

However carefully we plan, it's difficult to avoid gluts of certain crops in the garden. Vegetables can, of course, be frozen, but there are easy ways to turn them into delicious preserves. An abundance of homegrown summer fruits can be made into fragrant jams, and here I explain how achieve the perfect set.

PICKLES

Pickled vegetables, flavoured with herbs and spices, add a wonderful acidic crunch to dishes. They liven up snacks and sandwiches, and are a great addition to salads.

Makes enough to fill a 500ml (16fl oz) jar

400g (14oz) low-starch vegetables of your choice

250ml (9fl oz) vinegar (white/cider/malt)

250ml (9fl oz) water

30g (1oz) sugar

30g (1oz) salt

Spices: peppercorns, mustard seeds, coriander, or dill seeds work well

1. Wash and slice the vegetables into your desired thickness, and remember that thicker slices mean more crunch. If pickling very small cucumbers, leave them whole.

2. In a small saucepan, bring the vinegar, water, sugar, salt, and spices to a boil.

3. Place the vegetables into a sterilized jar and pour the hot pickling liquor over the top until tall the veg are completely covered.

4. Close the jar and leave it at room temperature for up to 4 weeks. Once opened, store in the fridge, where it will last for up to 3 months. If the ingredients are cut thinly, the pickle will be ready to eat after 24 hours.

Tip
When pickling mini-cucumbers (gherkins) (pictured right), I remove the flowering tip and add a tiny amount of chopped carrot. This preserves the satisfying "snap".

CHUTNEYS

Every gardener's best friend, chutney – or "glutney" as I like to call it – is a fantastic way to use an abundance of vegetables and fruit that don't freeze well (pictured below, right). For the spice blends (last three ingredients) see pp170–171.

Makes 4–5 350g (12oz) jars

1kg (2¼ lbs) of mixed vegetables and/or fruit

400g (14oz) tomatoes (red or green)

500ml (16fl oz) vinegar

250g (9oz) sugar

1 tbsp salt

2 tbsp panch phoron

1 tbsp all-purpose spice blend

1 tsp baharat

1. Wash and chop the vegetables into small pieces and place in a large stainless-steel saucepan.

2. Add the vinegar, sugar, salt, and the 3 spice blends, then bring the mixture to a boil over a medium heat, stirring frequently.

3. Reduce the heat to low and simmer the chutney for 1–2 hours, or until it has thickened and the vegetables are tender.

4. Allow the chutney to cool, then transfer it to sterilized jars. The chutney can be stored in the fridge for up to three months.

DRIED FRUIT AND VEG

Another way to preserve fruit and veg without using up freezer space is dehydration. Chillies and herbs are small so can simply be hung up in a well-ventilated space to dry naturally, but for watery ingredients like tomatoes and courgettes, a dehydrator is a good investment. If your budget is tight, simply slice ingredients very finely and dry on trays in a low oven. The instructions below are for using a dehydrator.

1. Wash fruit and vegetables before cutting into thin, uniformly sized pieces. Leave small ingredients, such as berries, whole.

2. Arrange everything on the dehydrator trays (tomatoes are pictured below).

3. Set the temperature of the dehydrator, then check on progress every three hours or so.

4. When the ingredients are dry and brittle (below, right), put them in an airtight container, adding a label and the date. Store at room temperature, out of direct sunlight, for up to a year.

Fruit leathers
Dried sheets of puréed fruit, these taste great and easy to make with a dehydrator.

1. Blend about 500g (1lb 2oz) of fruit and berries in a food processor until smooth (add water if necessary). Add honey or spices to taste.

2. Spread the resulting purée onto a silicone sheet, aiming for a thickness of around 5mm (¼in), then transfer the sheet to a dehydrator tray.

3. Set the machine to 60°C (140°F) and leave for 6–8 hours. The leather should be pliable but no longer sticky.

4. Once dry, remove the leather from the sheet and cut it into strips. Roll these up and store in an airtight

container. Eat within one month if stored at room temperature, or within six months if kept in the fridge.

Tip
Dehydrated fruits and berries add interest to teas and hot drinks, or you can include them in homemade granola or muesli mixes to add sweetness and flavour to breakfasts. Mushrooms also lend themselves very well to dehydration and can be added to pasta sauces and casseroles.

JAMS

Making jam is a wonderful way to preserve the sweetness of summer fruits, but jams can be deceptively tricky to get right. My tip for achieving a perfectly set jam is to make sure the total quantity of fruit includes 25 per cent that is underripe. Generally speaking, as fruit ripens, the sugar levels go up but the pectin levels – which help the jam to set, along with a small amount of citric acid – go down.

When making jam I start with the total weight of soft fruit then use it to calculate the amount of sugar and lemon juice using the following equation:

> Fruit (total weight)

> Jam sugar (50% of total fruit weight)

> Lemon juice (5% of total fruit weight)

The recipe below for strawberry jam will also work for other soft fruit including raspberries, currants, and gooseberries.

Strawberry jam

1kg (2¼ lbs) strawberries (including 250g/9oz unripe fruit)

500g (1lb 2oz) sugar

3 tbsp lemon juice

Makes approximately 2 x 500g (1lb 2oz) jars

1. Remove the strawberry leaves and stalks, and combine all the ingredients together in a bowl. Leave them to macerate overnight then clean and sterilize the jars ready for use the following day.

2. The next day, place a small plate in the fridge to chill for an hour.

3. Use your hands (or a potato masher) to squash everything together in the bowl, rather than spending time chopping up the fruit. This speedy method results in a rustic, uneven, but delicious jam.

4. Transfer the contents into a large pan and bring to a rapid boil, stirring frequently. As froth rises to the surface, scoop it off and discard.

5. When the mixture begins to sputter and bubble, and forms a glossy surface, place 1 tsp on the chilled plate then wait a minute and test by pushing the jam with your finger. When the surface wrinkles, the jam has reached setting point (pictured above). Take the jam off the heat and carefully transfer into sterilized jars. Now put the lids on tightly and allow the jars to cool at room temperature. The jam can be stored for up to nine months. Once opened, keep it in the fridge and use within a month.

Fermentation

The process of using naturally occurring cultures to unlock flavour and nutrients is becoming a popular way to boost gut health and extend the shelf life of our freshly grown produce. If you're new to fermentation or your previous attempts went horribly wrong, fear not. The following techniques are simple and effective.

LACTO-FERMENTATION

This wonderful fermenting technique (pictured left) is used to make kimchi and sauerkraut. It isn't complicated, and is suitable for virtually every crop in the garden. When added to a brine (salt and water), beneficial bacteria convert sugars in vegetables to lactic acid, which not only adds a tang but also acts as a preservative, like pickling. To limit the risk of spoilage, sanitize your equipment first and use a pH meter to check a level of acidity that indicates it's safe to eat. Discard any produce that is showing signs of mould or that smells unpleasant.

Makes enough to fill a 1.5 litre (2¾ pint) jar

1kg (2¼ lbs) vegetables of your choice

Enough water to cover the vegetables

Salt (2–5% of the total weight of vegetables and water, see step 4)

Whole spice/herb seeds

Sliced fresh ginger/garlic

Optional

Chilli powder to taste

1. Wash and then slice the vegetables into your desired thickness.

2. Weigh the sterilized jar then pack it full of the prepared vegetables, spices and herbs. I always include ginger root and/or garlic cloves as they impart great flavour and give a boost to beneficial bacteria. Leave a gap of 5cm (2in) at the top to allow for gas build-up.

3. Fill the jar with cold water until the ingredients are fully submerged, then weigh the jar again.

4. Subtract the weight of the empty jar from the full one then multiply the result by 0.02 to figure out how much salt you need. Add the salt , then close the lid and shake the jar to dissolve it.

5. Leave the jar out of direct sunlight for 3–7 days, opening the lid each day to allow the gas produced by fermentation to escape.

6. After a week, begin tasting the vegetables. When they are tangy enough, transfer the sealed jar to the fridge to slow the fermentation process, as well as preserve and develop the flavour. Use a pH meter to check levels. Owing to the salt content, the ferment is safe to eat at, or below, 4.6.

7. Use within 2 months.

"DRY" FERMENT

When making ferments using vegetables that have a very high proportion of water, such as courgettes, cabbage, and tomatoes, it isn't necessary to add liquid. Nor is it necessary when using grated vegetables and you can also massage salt into cabbage to draw out moisture. The salt alone will draw out the juices to produce a brine that has a delicious flavour.

For every 500g (1lb 2oz) of chopped or finely sliced vegetables you'll need 1½ tsp of salt.

1. Put the salt and vegetables into a sterilized jar.

2. Now weigh the ingredients down with glass or ceramic weight to make sure they stay well submerged below the brine. Leave for up to 2 days so the salt can draw out all the moisture.

3. From this point on, follow the method and storage for lacto-fermentation (see pp187–188).

Using fermented brine
The liquid extracted after adding salt to the veg in the "dry" method above is brimming with microbial activity and adds a huge amount of flavour and nutritional value when cooking and pickling.

Quick pickles Finely slice crunchy veg and store with a fully acidic fermenting liquor (pH 3.5 or lower) overnight in a fridge. The next day you'll have a delicious side dish, sandwich filler or salty crunch to add to salads.

Brine purée Blend a portion of the fermented veg (both with water and dry) and fermented brine together to make a sauce to liven up roast vegetables.

Butter glaze Add a knob of butter into a hot pan. Let it melt and bubble, but before it begins to brown, add the same amount of fermented brine. The pan will bubble

and steam for a minute before becoming a glaze to be brushed on vegetables or on meat before roasting.

WILD VINEGAR

Use this amazing technique to turn crops that are high in sugar into a full-flavoured vinegar with beneficial microbes. Homegrown and foraged fruit work well, as do tomatoes, and you can also add any leftover apple cores and peel to the mix.

Makes enough to fill a 1-litre (1¾-pint) jar

900g (2lbs) fruit or tomatoes

200g (7oz) raw cane sugar

1.8 litres (3 pints) water

150ml (5fl oz) raw* apple cider vinegar

* look for unpasteurized vinegar that contains the "mother" (beneficial bacteria)

1. First combine all the fruit/tomatoes and roughly mash or blend, then mix with the sugar and water and stir until the sugar is dissolved. Now transfer the contents into a large, sterilized jar. You don't need a lid.

2. Cover the jar with muslin or a tea towel, then secure with string or an elastic band. Store the jar out of direct sunlight.

3. Uncover and stir the contents every day with a sanitized wooden or plastic spoon. This introduces oxygen into the liquid, which stimulates fermentation. It also disturbs the surface to prevent mould growth. Continue to stir every day for two weeks.

4. Now, strain out the solids (pictured above) and transfer the vinegar to a new, clean jar. Cover as before and allow to ferment for another month. There's no need to stir the liquid.

5. The liquid should taste pleasantly sharp and fermentation should now be complete. Use a pH meter to check the reading is 2.5 or lower. If it isn't, you can lower pH levels further by adding strong white vinegar (6% acidity) or lemon juice

6. Transfer into bottles and either use right away or leave the vinegar to age and improve in flavour. To preserve the colour and flavour, store the bottled vinegar in the fridge and use within 6 months.

Drinks

Making delicious, healthy drinks from ingredients you've grown yourself is a truly rewarding experience. And, unlike the drinks in many self-sufficiency guides, my recipes don't involve brewing or long fermentations to produce alcohol. Instead, I'm sharing a selection of recipes the whole family can enjoy.

TEAS

Fresh flowers and herbs make warming teas (pictured right), or you can steep them overnight in the fridge for a refreshing drink on a hot day. Flowers are highly sensitive to temperature so the methods for hot and cold teas will yield dramatically different results. Always remove any pests from flowers and leaves beforehand.

Using a dehydrator on the lowest temperature, you can dry fresh flowers and herbs in just two hours, then store in airtight containers in a cool, dark place. If you don't have a dehydrator, make small bunches of flowers and/or herbs and hang them upside down, out of direct sunlight, to dry naturally. This process preserves the wonderful taste and aroma, allowing you to enjoy herbal teas all year round. To rehydrate, simply add freshly boiled water to the dried leaves or flowers and steep for five minutes. Add a teaspoon of honey or sugar to sweeten.

Hot tea

Add two handfuls of fresh or dried flowers and/or herbs to a small saucepan with 500ml (16fl oz) water and 1 tbsp honey or sugar. Simmer gently for five minutes, then strain the liquid into cups, and drink straight away.

Cold tea

Measure 500ml (16fl oz) of water into an airtight container, add honey or sugar to taste, and stir to dissolve. Using a pair of scissors, cut up the flowers and/or herbs to help release their natural aromas, and mix them into the liquid. Put a lid on and place the container in the fridge overnight to infuse (12 hours is ideal). Enjoy with ice on a hot summer day.

CORDIALS

Particularly juicy ingredients, such as berries and other soft fruit, make fantastic cordials (pictured opposite). For every 500g (1lb 2oz) of berries (fresh or frozen), you'll need 500ml (16fl oz) water, 350g (12oz) of sugar, and the rind and juice of a lemon. Not all cordials require lemon, but it adds a nice flavour and helps with preserving. Rhubarb also makes a good cordial, as do foraged wild fruits (see p194).

1. Add the berries (remove stalks) and the water to a large saucepan with the lemon rind and simmer for 30 minutes (pictured below).

2. Strain the mixture through a muslin cloth into a jug.

Don't press too hard or you'll add pulp as well as juice.

3. Clean the saucepan, pour the juice back into it, and return to a simmer.

4. Add the sugar and lemon juice, then stir until the sugar has dissolved.

5. Adjust the sweetness to taste, then pour the cordial into a 750ml- (1¾-pint) sterilized glass bottle, store in the fridge and use within three weeks.

Serving suggestions
For summer, serve cordials cold with crushed ice and a few fresh mint or lemon balm leaves. For a mulled winter cordial, put the liquid into a pan and add a cinnamon stick, a star anise, and a mace blade. Then bring the

liquid to a gentle simmer for 20–30 minutes.

Fresh flower cordial
Make a summery cordial from elder or other flowers by infusing 100g (3½oz) flowers in 825ml (1½ pints) of just-boiled water, 660g (1lb 7oz) sugar, and the rind and juice of a lemon. Let it sit at room temperature for 24 hours, then bottle and keep in the fridge.

SUMMER SODA

Fermenting the ingredients over three days extracts maximum flavour. This is a sophisticated, gin-like drink that is low in alcohol but with complexity and depth. Omit the sugar for a non-sparkling version.

2 litre (3½ pint) glass jar
Kitchen towel
String or elastic band
Square of muslin
Enough fresh mint, lemon balm, or lemon verbena leaves to fill the jar
200g (7oz) raw honey
Lemon, sliced
2 tsp sugar
Cold water

Optional
2.5cm (1in) fresh ginger, peeled and chopped

1. After sanitizing the jar, collect your chosen herbs and remove any pests.

2. Pack them into the jar with the fresh ginger, if using, but leave a gap of 5cm (2in) at the top for gas to build up during the fermentation process.

3. Add the honey, sliced lemon, and enough water to cover the herbs. You may need a weight to keep the ingredients submerged.

4. Cover the top of the jar with piece of kitchen towel and secure with string or an elastic band, then let it sit at room temperature and out of direct sunlight.

5. After three days, strain the liquid through the muslin and compost the leftover herbs. Transfer the strained liquid into two sterilized bottles, leaving a small gap at the top for gas build-up, then add 1 tsp sugar to each and shake to dissolve.

6. Place the bottles in the fridge for one to two days before drinking.

Foraged Food

Collecting edible, wild ingredients is a superb way to supplement meals and add extra nutrients for free. Make sure you forage on public, not private, land and never harvest too much or you may destroy the delicate balance of a fragile ecosystem.

Common foraged ingredients are listed in the chart opposite according to the month when they are most plentiful, with suggestions on how to cook with them. But before you go foraging, familiarize yourself with each plant, either online or consult a field guide. Also, ensure you can identify potentially harmful lookalikes, such as lily of the valley, which resembles wild garlic but the leaves have no onion scent.

Month	Plant	Part used	Flavour	How to use
January	Nettle	Leaves	Spinach with a kick	Make a tea from fresh or dried leaves. Add young leaves to soups, scrambled eggs, and quiches.
February	Chickweed	Leaves	Like lettuce	Blend into pesto or soups. Use as a garnish for winter salads.
March	Wild sorrel	Leaves	Lemony, very sour	Use only in small amounts. Blend into soups for a lemony kick.
April	Wild garlic	Leaves, stem, flowers, seeds	Delicate to strong onion	Treat leaves as baby spinach and add to pies and quiches; ferment in kimchi. Seeds make good caper substitutes and flowers can be added to salads.
May	Hawthorn	Flowers	Mild marzipan	Great in cordials.
June	Elder	Flowers	Citrusy lemon/ floral pear	Make into a delicate cordial or tea (see pp190–193).
July	Bilberry	Ripe berries	Sweet and rich	Cook and turn into cordials, compôtes, jams, sauces, and sweet pie filling.
August	Elderberry	Ripe berries	Tart	Cook to remove toxins and turn into cordials, jams, wines, syrup, and ketchup.
September	Hawthorn, rosehips (pictured left)	Ripe berries	Tart but slightly sweet	Cook hawthorn then remove the seeds and turn into jelly, tea, or syrup. Use roships to make jams, cordials, and sodas but always remove the seeds first.
October	Damson, sloes	Ripe fruit	Sour plum	Cook damsons and make jams, pies, and chutney; infuse damsons and sloes in either gin or vodka.
November	Sweet chestnut	Shelled nuts	Earthy and sweet	Eat freshly roasted or add roast nuts to pies, stuffing, and soups.
December	Marsh samphire	Stem tips	Crisp and salty	Steam and stir into lemony pasta or buttery potato dishes.

Growing Skills

40

Sowing

In general, the most cost-effective way to raise vegetables is from seed. The two most common methods are direct sowing, or sowing in pots and modules, but of course, there are exceptions. Raising heat-loving aubergines, peppers, and chillies from seed can be expensive because they need warmth and light early in the season. Buying a few seedlings instead is often a cheaper and easier option.

DIRECT SOWING

The clue is in the name: you sow seeds directly where they are to grow and the method is very simple (pictured opposite, bottom).

1. Tie a length of string to two sticks, stretch it out and mark out the row.

2. With the back of a rake handle, make a trench in the soil at the correct depth for the seed.

3. Sow the seeds along the base of the trench.

4. Gently cover over and pat down so the seeds make good contact with the soil.

5. Give the row a good soaking (or sow a few hours before heavy rain).

Seedbed sowing
When sowing leeks and stemmed brassicas, such as broccoli and kale, I prefer to start them off in a seedbed so I can propagate many plants in a small space. When the seedlings are growing well and have true leaves, they are lifted and planted, at a wider spacing, into their final home.

SOWING IN POTS AND MODULES

Starting seeds off under cover allows you to raise plants while you wait for warmer weather. Seedlings that have been growing in pots or modules (pictured opposite, top) will also be ready for transplanting as soon as the previous crop has been harvested. Whether you sow in pots or modules, the method is the same.

1. Fill pots or modules with compost (peat-free multipurpose or seed

compost) and press down firmly. Now top up the module with compost

2. Water before you sow so the holes you will make for the seeds don't collapse in on themselves.

3. Use a dibber or your finger to make holes at the correct depth for each seed (pictured above, top).

4. Sow your seeds and then cover with extra compost. Press down lightly.

5. Label and give the seeds a final water.

Transplanting

When pricking out young seedlings, always hold them carefully by a leaf, so you don't damage the fragile stem. With bigger seedlings, whether grown in modules, pots, or in a seedbed, hold them by the rootball or the leaves, and give them plenty of water before and after transplanting.

PRICKING OUT

The goal of pricking out is to germinate lots of seedlings using minimal compost. You then select the best seedlings to grow on individually in larger modules, before you transplant them into their growing postion.

1. Fill small pots or larger-celled modules with compost.

2. Use a seed label to gently remove each seedling from the seed tray, when you notice the first two true leaves have appeared.

3. Hold the seedling by a leaf while you make a small hole with a pencil in the compost.

4. Bury the seedling so that just 5–10mm (¼–½in) of stem is visible below the leaves, then water gently.

MODULE-GROWN SEEDLINGS

1. Always stand module trays in 2.5cm (1in) of water for 5–10 minutes to ensure the seedlings soak up water before transplanting.

2. Use a finger to push the seedlings up out of the cell, and hold them by the rootball (pictured top left).

3. With your fingers or a dibber, make a hole in the soil slightly deeper than the rootball, and place the seedling in it (pictured top right).

4. Push firmly down around the seedling with your hands (pictured opposite) and water it in. Planting a little deeper allows the water to pool around the stem then go straight to the roots.

LARGE SEEDLINGS

1. Before transplanting large seedlings, such as brassicas, grown in in 7–9cm (2¾–3½in) pots, water each seedling in its pot.

2. Use a trowel to make a hole the same width but 1½ times deeper than the pot, then add a generous handful of homemade compost to the base of the hole.

3. With one hand covering the top of the seedling, turn the pot upside down and tap the base gently to release the rootball (pictured opposite).

4. Place the seedling in the hole, then water in before using your hands to firm around the sides then press down around the roots.

SEEDLINGS GROWN IN A SEED BED

1. Using a fork, gently lift seedlings, such as leeks out of the seed bed. Some soil will still be clinging to their roots.

2. Soak them in a bucket of water for 10 minutes then gently shake to disentangle the roots and separate the plants (pictured below).

3. Use a dibber to create a hole in the soil the length of

the wet roots, and drop a seedling into each hole.

4. Now fill the hole to the top with water, then tamp down the soil, and firm it around the seedling.

These bare-root seedlings may wilt, but perk up again by day three.

TIP

When transplanting brassicas and tomatoes that have at least five to six true leaves, bury the plants deeply so the first set is just above soil level. This promotes strong not leggy growth, as well as stability.

Watering

The following watering advice should be taken as a guide rather than a set of hard-and-fast rules. Essentially, watering is about ensuring plants stay hydrated so they aren't stressed. As long as you make sure you don't let your plants wilt, you're well on your way to success.

SEEDLINGS

Young seedlings are very fragile. They require gentle watering, which is best done from the base. Fill a leak-proof tray with 3–4cm (1¼–1½in) of water and carefully place the module trays or pots in the tray. The compost will act as a wick, drawing water upwards. After 10 minutes, seedlings will be well hydrated and the trays can be placed back onto the shelf. Water whenever the top 2cm (¾in) of compost feels dry.

Potted seedlings

Base watering is always the best option for seedlings that have been in their pots for at least four weeks. And it's also the best method for seedlings of any age. After overhead watering, the compost may look moist, but could still be bone dry just under the surface. If you have several trays of seedlings and not enough time to base water, simply water overhead once, then repeat after 15 minutes. Water whenever the top 2–3cm (¾–1¼in) of compost feels dry.

Direct-sown seeds and seedlings

Keep the ground where you've sown seeds moist, but not saturated. The plank method (see p31) is really effective for retaining moisture, and once germination has occurred you simply remove the plank. For the first four weeks after germination, water seedlings whenever the top 2–3cm (¾–1¼in) of soil feels dry.

MATURE PLANTS

With well-developed roots that can access moist soil well below the surface, mature plants don't need watering as regularly as seedlings. But there are two instances when mature plants definitely need water: firstly, when the top 5cm (2in) of soil feels bone dry; and secondly when there has been no rain for a week and none forecast for the next few days. Always water mature plants as close to the base of their stem as possible. It's the best way to get water directly to the roots, where it's needed.

Perennials

These hardy plants need little water unless the weather is extremely dry. Give them a deep watering every two weeks in very dry spells. After watering perennials, or immediately after rain, mulch around them with a 5cm (2in) layer of grass clippings, leaves, or woodchip. This helps to reduce evaporation and retains moisture.

Soaker hose

This efficient irrigation method is ideal for crops, such as rows of tomato plants, growing in the polytunnel. Water seeps from the hose directly into the soil, and then down to the roots. Setting up this type of system can save you a lot of time, especially if you link the hose up to a timer for automatic watering.

Tip
Chlorine in tap water can damage soil microbes. If you store tap water in an outside tank, let it sit for 24 hours before using to water plants. This will give the chlorine time to disperse.

Minimal Disturbance Gardening

This term, MDG for short, describes my approach to growing nutritious food while improving the long-term health of the soil. MDG doesn't have to mean no-dig; neither does it involve a hard-and-fast set of rules. Flexibility is key and the degree of "minimal disturbance" you choose will depend on personal circumstances and your experience and understanding of your own garden.

PRINCIPLES AND PRACTICE

I've put together a few guiding principles and listed them here along with some practical applications:

1. Assess before action
When planning a specific task that may require soil disturbance, first assess all available options. Now consider which one will be most suitable and beneficial, then act accordingly. If the soil is compacted at the start of a growing season, for example, you could use a broad fork to loosen it.

2. Ecosystem emphasis
When, like me, you view the garden as a complete ecosystem, what is happening above ground is as important as what is going on below. Promote biodiversity by growing pollinator-friendly plants, and apply homemade biological amendments (see p208) to boost beneficial microbes.

3. Responsible resourcing
Use local and sustainable resources to save costs. For example, instead of buying compost to create new beds, try trench composting. Dig a trench around 50cm (20in) deep, fill up to

two-thirds with veg scraps, then cover and plant on top. The material will break down to provide organic matter and add fertility. Also, if the budget is tight, save money by not buying organic seeds

4. Dynamic crop polyculture
Aim to have a diversity of annual crops growing in the same location throughout the growing season. This helps to prevent a build-up of crop-specific issues (pests, diseases, and nutritional deficiencies) while increasing garden productivity and resilience.

Techniques such as intercropping, succession planting, and companion planting all contribute.

5. Continuous soil cover
To protect the soil, try to keep it covered as much as possible. Planting cover crops such as phacelia, protects ground over winter, before the crop is cut and allowed to return to the soil. Covering empty raised beds with breathable materials, such as cardboard (pictured above), also minimizes exposure to the elements.

MDG and self-sufficiency
One of the biggest challenges gardeners face on their self-sufficiency journey is having enough compost. It's expensive to buy in and you always need to be on top of making your own. The MDG approach offers a whole suite of alternative ways to increase fertility, such as the trench method under 3 (opposite). Also, lacking compost doesn't mean you can't grow hungry crops, such as pumpkins or tomatoes. Bury a few large handfuls of kitchen scraps two months

prior to planting out, use a stick to mark the spots, then transplant the seedlings into the same locations.

MDG is an adaptable approach to growing that will save you money and can be tailored to your own needs as a gardener. Its focus on practical, self-reliant gardening strategies makes its methods ideal for those seeking a sustainable, self-sufficient lifestyle.

Amendments

Amendments are natural, non-invasive preparations that boost the health of your plants and increase their resistance to attack by pests and diseases. The four amendments I recommend here are easy and inexpensive to make at home, and two of them will also improve soil health and quality.

LAB

Lactic acid bacteria (LAB) is a Korean Natural Farming microbial amendment that has a whole range of amazing benefits. I'm sharing detailed Instructions so you can make your own, and it has a fridge life of up to six months.

Added to the compost heap, LAB will accelerate the decomposition process and eliminate the whiff of smelly compost. Sprayed in diluted form onto leaves, LAB helps protect young plants from diseases, such as powdery mildew; you can also water it onto your beds. LAB also improves soil structure, increases water retention, and breaks down nutrients so they are readily taken up by plants.

Making your own involves two stages: preparing the rice-water stock, then adding milk to feed the lactic acid bacteria, which multiply in their millions.

Stage 1 Making stock

250g (9oz) uncooked organic white rice

250ml (8fl oz) water

250ml (8fl oz) glass jar

Rubber band and piece of muslin-type cloth (for lid)

2 large mixing bowls

Sieve

1. Place the sieve over one of the large mixing bowls, add the rice, and pour the water over.

2. Transfer the sieve with rice to sit over the other mixing bowl, then pour the water from the first bowl over it. Repeat 8–10 times and notice the water turning cloudier as the starch is washed from the rice.

3. Pour the cloudy water into a glass jar, cover with the cloth, which allows air into the mix, and secure with a rubber band.

4. Leave somewhere indoors out of direct sunlight, such as a kitchen countertop, for 3 days. Bacteria will feed on the starch and the stock will smell like old vase water.

Stage 2 Feeding the bacteria

1.5 litres (2¾ pints) whole organic cow's milk

2-litre (4-pint) glass jar

1-litre (2-pint) glass jar

Fine sieve

1. Discard the top filmy layer in the stock jar using a soup spoon. Pour the clear liquid beneath into the larger glass jar and also discard the sediment left in the bottom of the stock jar.

2. Pour the milk on top of the stock and mix.

3. Reuse the cloth and rubber band from the stock jar and leave in the same location for five to six days.

4. The liquid will now have separated into LAB serum (whey) and curds (pictured below). And yes, you can make cheese with the curds!

5. Using a fine sieve, separate the liquid from the curds and pour it into the second clean jar.

6. Label the jar and store in the fridge for up to 6 months. Use, diluted in a ratio of 1:1,000 or 2 teaspoons in a 10-litre (2-gallon) watering can.

JMS

JADAM Microbial Solution (JMS) is a fantastic liquid amendment that employs leaf mould as an inoculant (activator). One batch will produce quantities of beneficial microbes that you can add to your soil. These microbes improve soil structure, break down nutrients so plants can access them, and protect plant roots. The solution is most effective when applied to the soil a couple of weeks before you plant out a crop.

Once the crop is growing well, water with diluted JMS for an added boost to soil and plant health. Microbe species are sensitive to temperature so if you plan to use JMS in the polytunnel, I recommend assembling the ingredients and making the solution in the tunnel itself.

Making JMS

50-litre (11-gallon) bucket with handle and lid

2 medium boiled potatoes

Handful of leaf mould

1 tsp sea salt

Square of muslin-type cloth or hessian (50 x 50cm/20 x 20in)

String

1. Fill the bucket with rainwater.

2. Place the potatoes and leaf mould in the centre of the fabric square.

3. Bring the 4 corners together and use the string to tie into a small bag.

4. Tie another piece of string to the bucket handle and attach it to the bag, ensuring the bag is submerged but doesn't sink to the bottom. If your bucket has no handle, place the end of the string under a brick.

5. Add the sea salt to the water then firmly massage the bag so the potatoes and leaf mould are throughly mashed together. The water will turn cloudy.

6. Loosely place a lid on the bucket and leave in place for 3-5 days.

7. When you see white bubbles on the surface of the liquid, the JMS is ready for use. Don't wait until the bubbles turn brown as the microbes will be less active.

8. Dilute the JMS in a ratio of 1:10 for use on bare soil and 1:20 on planted ground.

PLANT "TEA"

A simple liquid feed couldn't be easier to make and the plants will be growing around or near your garden. Pick comfrey, nettles, borage, dock, thistles, grass, and dandelion foliage, and either create a balanced mix or focus on just one ingredient for a specific purpose. Comfrey tea, for example, is ideal for tomatoes and squash.

Fill a bucket with your chosen plant material, add enough water to cover, then leave somewhere out of the rain for two weeks (pictured opposite, top). Use fresh feed diluted in a ratio of 1:10 and water on weekly to give crops a general boost (pictured opposite, below). If the feed is more than 4 weeks old, dilute in a ratio of 1:20.

Tip

If you haven't made a liquid amendment, the next best thing would be to buy organic seaweed feed.

PLANT CONCENTRATES

Nettles, comfrey, borage, and dock are particularly high in minerals and make fantastic concentrated feeds. Gather enough of your

chosen plant leaves (either of one plant or a mix of plants) to fill a bucket or tub and pack them down using a stone as a weight. No need to add water. Cover loosely with a lid and leave for at least two to three months. Tip the resulting dark liquid into a jar, then dilute in a ratio of 1:100 (100ml in a 10-litre can) and apply at the base of your plants fortnightly.

Late summer is a great time to start off concentrates, because it allows the foliage to break down over the winter. The concentrates are then ready for use by the start of the next growing season. The thick, syrupy liquid can be stored in plastic bottles) or glass jars in a cool, dark place.

Weeding and Protecting

Weeds will compete with growing crops for water and nutrients but regular weeding will ensure these tenacious plants don't out-compete your crops. A hard frost early in the season, on the other hand, can decimate young plants overnight so I employ frost-protection strategies that help to safeguard tender plants.

WEEDING

Given its small area, the self-sufficiency garden is easily manageable once you adopt a simple weeding regime. Aim to walk around and between the beds every two to three days, hand-pulling any weeds that have made an appearance. Those that have escaped your notice and gained a foothold can easily be uprooted with a hand fork.

Use a hoe
A long-handled oscillating or push-pull hoe is my favourite tool for keeping down weeds, and hoeing is gentler on the back than bending down to hand weed (pictured opposite). Choose a hoe with a narrow head that can be used between rows of crops, running the blade 1–2cm (½–¾in) below the soil so you slice off the weed roots. Ideally, hoe in the morning on a sunny day or when there's a wind so the weeds wilt and die on the surface, saving you the bother of picking them up.

Winter
During the colder months when we're in the garden less, weeds will still be appearing and can soon take hold. Cover any bare ground with a couple of layers of cardboard weighted down with stones, then remove it the following spring and compost the cardboard.

CROP PROTECTION

The key to minimizing cold-weather damage is to work around the average date of the last spring frosts in your area, and keep a close eye on the weather. However, if a frost is forecast and you've already planted out tender veg, you can still protect them overnight using one of the three methods outlined below.

Fleece
Whenever there is a risk of frost (my rule of thumb is a night-time temperature

forecast of 4°C/39°F or below), drape some thick horticultural fleece (30g type) over crops such as new potatoes. Secure the edges with stones or wood to stop it blowing away. Thick fleece acts as a big, warm blanket and is a good investment that will last many seasons. And because fleece allows light through to the crops below, you can leave it in place for as long as needed. But if funds are tight, an old sheet spread over short sticks to keep it off the foliage will also do the job.

Bottle cloches
Cut the base from a large plastic bottle and place it over a tender young plant, such as a courgette, to keep frost at bay. If possible, put the bottle cloches in place in the afternoon so the air inside has time to warm up. The top can be unscrewed for ventilation the next day. This is a great method for bringing on seedlings faster during cooler weather, regardless of frost risk.

Cardboard boxes
For inexpensive, temporary protection of recently transplanted squash, for example, use upturned cardboard boxes. When overnight frost is forecast, place the box over the plant in the early evening and weigh it down with a stone if there's a wind. Remove the box the following morning.

Resources

GROWING

Seeds
Real Seeds realseeds.co.uk
Vital Seeds vitalseeds.co.uk
Kings Seeds kingsseeds.com
Wales Seed Hub seedhub.wales

Peat-free compost
Melcourt melcourt.co.uk
Dalefoot dalefootcomposts.co.uk

Seed trays, modules, and containers
Containerwise containerwise.co.uk

Polytunnels
First Tunnels firsttunnels.co.uk

Tools
Gardena gardena.com/uk
Niwaki niwaki.com

Footwear
Muck Boot Company muckbootcompany.co.uk

Plants
Urban Herbs urban-herbs.co.uk

Books
Food for Free Richard Mabey
Gaia's Garden Toby Hemenway
Hot Beds Jack First
How to Grow Winter Vegetables Charles Dowding
Practical Self-Sufficiency Dick and
   James Strawbridge

River Cottage Handbook series
The New Complete Book of Self-Sufficiency
   John Seymour

Recommended YouTube channels
Charles Dowding
David the Good
Edible Acres
Gaz Oakley
Huw Richards
Liz Zorab – Byther Farm
Freedom Forest Life

FOOD

Books
Any book by Hugh Fearnley-Whittingstall
Salt, Fat, Acid, Heat Samin Nosrat
Tartine Bread Chad Robertson
The Complete Vegetable Cookbook
   James Strawbridge
The Larousse Book of Bread Eric Kayser
The Nature of Food Sam Cooper
The New Wildcrafted Cuisine Pascal Baudar

Recipes online
@chef.sam.black on Instagram

Equipment
pH meter (inexpensive works well)
Kilner kilnerjar.co.uk (preserving jars)
Scanpan scanpanuk.co.uk (pans)
Zyliss zyliss.co.uk (pans)

Index

Acknowledgments

Thanks from Huw and Sam
We would love to thank the DK team for their belief in our idea for this book from day one. Firstly, to our publisher, Katie Cowan, for giving us the green light, followed by Ruth, Max, Glenda, and, of course, Lucy for turning our idea into a physical book. Thank you, also, to Laura Macdougall from United Agents for your incredible support.

And to our colleagues, Stacey Bell for being the organizational glue that holds us together and Neil Jones for being our garden gnome – never change!

Huw's acknowledgments
Thanks to my family: Steven, Clarrissa, and Fflur, thanks for being my biggest fan club; Sam Cooper for having to put up with my constant torrent of ideas and questions; all my followers – nothing would be possible without you, especially this book; and finally, to my local café, Medina, for being my writing retreat.

Sam's acknowledgments
Thanks to my family and loved ones: Wai Yan, Jane, Margaret, and Ben for their infinite patience, support, and inspiration, and for always making time for good, honest food; Huw Richards, for growing all the wonderful produce; all my followers, who are the best possible community of foodies a man could belong to; and the many chefs and bakers I've had the pleasure of working with and learning from.

Publisher's acknowledgments
DK would like to thank Daniel Crisp for the illustration on page 24, Dawn Titmus for the proofread, Lisa Footitt for creating the index, and Steve Crozier for repro work.

About the Authors

Huw Richards is a permaculturalist, digital creator, and co-director for Regenerative Media based in mid-west Wales. Aged 12, he created his own YouTube channel about growing your own food. He now has over 750,000 YouTube subscribers and his videos have collectively been viewed more than 85 million times. Huw sets out to make growing your own food as accessible as possible for as many people as possible. He has already authored three books with DK, *Veg in One Bed* (2019), *Grow Food For Free* (2020), and *The Vegetable Grower's Handbook* (2022). Huw can also be found on Instagram @huwsgarden.

Sam Cooper originally worked as a chef in multiple kitchens in Shropshire and mid-west Wales before meeting Huw Richards and becoming co-director for Regenerative Media. He has a following of over 500,000 as @chef.sam.black on Instagram, where he shares videos using homegrown, seasonal, and foraged produce with a focus on fermenting. Sam wrote the In the Kitchen chapter of *The Self-Sufficiency Garden* and published his first book *The Nature of Food* in 2022.

DK LONDON
Editorial Manager Ruth O'Rourke
Project Editor Lucy Philpott
Senior Designer Glenda Fisher
Design Assistant Izzy Poulson
Production Editor David Almond
Senior Production Controller Stephanie McConnell
DTP and Design Coordinator Heather Blagden
Jacket Designer Izzy Poulson
Jacket and Sales Material Coordinator Emily Cannings
Art Director Maxine Pedliham
Publishing Director Katie Cowan

Editor Anna Kruger
Designer Matt Cox at Newman+Eastwood Ltd
Illustrator Tobatron
Jacket Illustrator Sam Cooper

First published in Great Britain in 2024 by
Dorling Kindersley Limited
DK, One Embassy Gardens, 8 Viaduct Gardens,
London, SW11 7BW

The authorised representative in the EEA is
Dorling Kindersley Verlag GmbH. Arnulfstr. 124,
80636 Munich, Germany

A CIP catalogue record for this book
is available from the British Library.
ISBN: 978-0-2416-4143-9

Printed and bound in Slovakia

www.dk.com